FIVE FACES OF AMERICA

An intimate account of the spiritual journeys
of five Americans, whose varied ethnic and
cultural backgrounds demonstrate that God
is truly no respecter of persons, and that His
Holy Spirit indwells and guides the lives
of all true believers in Jesus Christ.

By

H. Dane Harris, Sr.

xulon PRESS

Table Of Contents

Dedication

This book is dedicated to the memory of my late parents, Olean Moss Harris and Howard Clayton Harris, and to my immediate family for their love, support and dedication to leading spiritually directed lives. They include my wife, Constance Miller Harris, and our four sons and their families. They are:

Ashley Stuart Harris
H. Dane Harris, Jr.,
Mark Miller Harris and his wife, Lori, and
William Clayton Harris, his wife, Jeanne,
and our grandchildren, Madeleine Nicole Harris and Evan Clayton Harris.

My prayer is that the Holy Spirit will permanently indwell their hearts and lives, assuring their inheritance of the Kingdom of God, to reign as priests and kings with Christ upon His return, as promised in the scriptures.

Acknowledgments

I wish to acknowledge all whose cooperation and assistance have made this work possible.

The leadership of the Holy Spirit in my own life has been the primary motivator in undertaking the writing of this book. For more than two decades I have wrestled with the concept of such a book. Finally, I feel that God's spiritual inspiration has made it a reality. Without the guidance of the Holy Spirit, such an effort would be of little consequence. The book's sole purpose is to help both believers in Christ and those who have not made a profession of faith, to better understand God's desire that all might come to know Him and through the indwelling of His Holy Spirit, to live according to His commandments, ultimately becoming heirs to His Kingdom upon Christ's promised return.

The "Five Faces," whose spiritual journeys illustrate the power of the Holy Spirit to direct the lives of believers in Christ, are due special thanks for their willingness to share their intimate, personal stories, and for their patience. Vina Harvey Coleman, Raul A. Gonzalez, Rev. Bertram Bobb, Don G. Kaspar and William O. Bolen have been faithful and forthcoming in sharing their innermost feelings and search for spiritual direction for their lives. All have been an inspiration to me and I pray that their stories may inspire others, as well.

The Choctaw Nation of Oklahoma and its official newspaper, BISHINIK, have provided key resource material, as have the authors of other publications listed in the bibliography. The Austin Baptist Association also provided information and support in conducting some of the interviews.

My wife, Connie, has given helpful suggestions and input during the preparation of the manuscript. Joe L. Hanson, a lay leader and a trustee of Dallas Theological Seminary, has provided critiques and counsel during its preparation. And my son, Dane Harris, Jr., Esq., has assisted me in some of my travels and research.

To all of these and to others who have encouraged this undertaking in a variety of ways, I express my deep personal gratitude.

Bibliography

Texas Secretary of State, Elections Section, 1994 Primary and General Election Results

A History of the Kaspar Family, 1740-1980, by Edgar Herbert Kaspar

The History of Kaspar Wire Works, Inc., by Arthur H. Kaspar and Don G. Kaspar

Choctaw Nation of Oklahoma, Language Department, Public Information Office

An Introduction To The Choctaw Language, a paper by Todd Downing

BISHINIK, official newspaper of the Choctaw Nation of Oklahoma

Choctaw Nation History, The Rise and Fall of The Choctaw Republic by Angie Debo, University of Oklahoma Press

Old Choctaw Beliefs, a paper by Jesse Ben

The Choctaw, by Jesse O. McKee, one of the series on "Indians of North America," Frank W. Porter III, general editor

Choctaw Hymn Book, published by Global Bible Society, Asheville, N.C.

World Book Encyclopedia

"Africans In America," a documentary series by Public Broadcasting System/WGBH

Texas Tech University *Law Review, Faith and The Law Symposium*, Volume 27, Number Three, 1996

The John Pirtle Family From The Lincoln Country of Kentucky, written and compiled by Henry M. Johnson, Esq., and Henry J. Tilford, Esq.

The Ryrie Study Bible, New American Standard Edition, Moody Press, 1978

The Holy Bible, Pilgrim Edition, King James Version, Oxford University Press, 1952

Foreword

America is a land of many faces. There are faces of many shapes, sizes and colors. They represent a myriad of cultural and ethnic backgrounds. And their values, personalities and tastes are as varied as the leaves on a tree.

They are drawn from every continent and every principality on the earth in search of opportunity for expression, for individual freedom and the hope of a better life for those who will follow.

There is no typical face among them. However, there are similarities, which transcend the many differences. These are similarities of the heart, mind and soul. They are similarities of values, of yearnings and of dreams.

This, then, is the story of five of those faces. While unique and varied in terms of origin and background, they represent basic threads in the fabric of America. Indeed, their stories are the story of America, a land, which challenges the mind and frees the heart and soul of every individual to achieve whatever he or she can dream.

Theirs also are stories of faith. Man, after all, is a spiritual being and without faith in God, there can be no fulfillment of his innate yearning for meaning to life and eternal existence. Thus, one universal trait shared by all is a longing for fulfillment of the soul, a purpose for life and eternal salvation.

So, these are faces of believers in the Christian faith,

which has been a driving force in the establishment of America. From the emergence of native tribes on the North American continent thousands of years ago, to the Sixteenth Century Spanish conquistadors and later, the European pilgrims who began settlement on the eastern edge of the continent in the early Seventeenth Century, there has been a consistent longing for spiritual freedom and purpose for life. And the fact that the quest for material gain was an objective in the adventures of the conquistadors and early explorers should not obscure the spiritual impact their explorations would have.

One of the "Five Faces" belongs to a Native American, whose ancestors inhabited the continent for centuries before the arrival of the conquistadors and pilgrims from Europe, carrying the banner of religious freedom and evangelistic fervor, along with the quest for material wealth and power.

A second face represents the fastest growing ethnic group in America, Hispanics, whose ancestry predates the western European settlers who are the focus of so much of the early history of America.

A third face is that of an African American, descended from slaves who were brought to America against their will.

Another face is that of a descendant of Europeans, whose early forebears migrated to America as part of the fervor, beginning in the Seventeenth Century, to evangelize the New World.

And a fifth face represents generic America, the melting pot of many different Anglo-Saxon-Celtic strains represented in main stream America today.

All of the faces personify the American dream, giving testimony to the fact that spiritual faith, individual initiative, and a commitment to values higher than oneself are foundation stones for successful living, irrespective of ethnic origin, cultural background, or economic status.

The fact that all five faces are representative of the

Christian faith is not intended as disregard for those of other faiths represented in the spiritual fabric of America. Rather, these are stories about the practical application of the Holy Spirit in the lives of representative individuals who have professed faith in Jesus Christ as their Lord and Savior and who have claimed His promise to send a Holy Comforter to guide them. The stories are also testimony to the strength and diversity of a nation, which empowers every individual to make decisions about religious faith according to personal conscience, rather than by government edict.

The accounts of their spiritual journeys are their own. They are based, for the most part, upon personal interviews and recollections, in some instances amplified by personal histories or genealogical records. But the stories are not intended to be historical records as such, though every effort has been made to assure their historical accuracy. Rather, their objective is to serve as intimate, personal accounts of the power of the Holy Spirit in the lives of representative individuals who have claimed His promise that the Holy Comforter would indwell their hearts and provide comfort and guidance in their daily lives.

The stories are as unique as the individuals who tell them. Hopefully, they will serve as examples of confident living and as inspiration to both those who are seeking to make their Christian walk more meaningful and to those who have yet to make a spiritual commitment.

Introduction

The Holy Spirit

The concept of the Holy Spirit is perhaps the most mystifying and least understood aspect of the Christian experience.

Some Christian ministers seem reluctant to speak about the Holy Spirit. And many who do proclaim Him from the pulpit, describe Him in the Biblical context of the "Holy Ghost," which has a mystical, even surreal connotation to many non-believers and some believers, as well.

Christian is a term which literally means "Christ's one." It was first used to describe believers in the Lord Jesus Christ in the First Century Church at Antioch, on the northeastern shore of the Mediterranean Sea, where the Apostle Paul would later begin his missionary journeys. (Acts 11:26)

While Christian was the name first given to believers in Christ by the secular world, which acknowledged only external manifestations, it more accurately describes those who have had a personal, inner experience with God, working through the crucifixion and resurrection of His Son, Jesus Christ, and the indwelling of His Holy Spirit in the hearts of believers in Christ.

Among many theologians and Christian denominations, the Holy Spirit has been interpreted as a third person of the Godhead. Hence, the concept of the Holy Trinity, …God the Father, God the Son and God the Holy Spirit. The Holy Spirit is portrayed in certain instances as a force or power utilized by God the Father and His son, Jesus Christ, to deal with the hearts and minds of His faithful. The first chapter of the book of Luke, verses 34 and 35, reveal that the Holy Spirit was the power used by God the Father to beget His son Jesus Christ in the womb of the virgin Mary. So, it was through the power of the Holy Spirit that God became flesh in the person of Jesus Christ.

It is revealing to note that the Apostle Paul, in numerous letters to the New Covenant Christians in the First Century, did not address the Holy Spirit as a part of the Triune or Godhead, in the same way that he addressed the Father and the Son, Jesus Christ. This is also true of the Apostle John in writing the books of I John and II John in the New Testament. However, the purpose here is not to engage in any theological debate about the Trinity. Rather, it is to emphasize the reality of the Holy Spirit, His divine, compelling, and transcendent nature, and how He works in the lives of believers in Christ.

While some regard the Holy Spirit as primarily a New Testament phenomenon, a fulfillment of Christ's promise to send a Holy Comforter to indwell His followers after His crucifixion, resurrection and ascension into Heaven, there are numerous references to the Holy Spirit in the Old Testament. Examples are II Kings, Psalm 104 and Genesis 6, which reference the Holy Spirit as the power by which God creates and through which He deals with and guides His people. However, accounts of visitations by the Holy Spirit in the Old Testament describe events that were temporary in nature. It was not until Christ was crucified, resurrected and ascended into Heaven that the Holy Spirit would permanently indwell all believers.

The New Testament contains numerous accounts of the Holy Spirit anointing and indwelling the hearts of believers. The first chapter of the Acts of the Apostles gives an account of Jesus, following His crucifixion and resurrection, predicting a time when believers would be baptized with the Holy Spirit. This visitation of the Holy Spirit is vividly described in subsequent portions of The Acts. The second chapter of Acts tells of the Jews at Pentecost professing faith in Christ and receiving the Holy Spirit in a most dramatic way, testimony to the world of the reality and power of the Spirit. Verse four recounts "And they were filled with the Holy Ghost and began to speak with other tongues, as the Spirit gave them utterance." According to Luke, the author, there was a mighty rushing wind from Heaven, punctuated with tongues of fire, which sat upon the disciples, each of whom began to speak in other languages. And as the people, who were assembled there from every part of the then known world, heard the disciples speaking in their native tongues, they understood that this truly was the work of the Lord. Three thousand persons were converted and baptized as a result of this visitation of the Spirit, marking the establishment of God's only earthly institution, the church. Acts also recounts an incident where Philip, one of the first deacons of the early church, along with the martyr Stephen, was on a preaching mission to the city of Samaria. A number of people accepted Christ and were baptized, but it was not until the disciples Peter and John laid their hands on the converts that they actually received the Holy Spirit. The account also tells of Simon, a sorcerer, who had been converted, attempting to buy this power from the disciples with money, but being rebuked.

Perhaps the most dramatic and personal account of an individual's encounter with God, followed by the indwelling of the Holy Spirit, is the Damascus Road experience of Saul of Tarsus, recorded in the ninth chapter of Acts. Ironically,

Saul, the infamous persecutor of Christians, was carrying letters to the synagogues in Damascus authorizing him to arrest and return to Jerusalem any followers of Christ, when he was struck by a bright light from Heaven. At the same moment, he heard a voice from Heaven ask, "Saul, Saul, why are you persecuting me?" To which Saul replied, "Who art thou, Lord?" And the answer came back, "I am Jesus whom you are persecuting." Yielding to the Lord, Saul asked, "What wilt thou have me do?" The voice from Heaven then instructed him to go into the city and wait for guidance.

Having been temporarily blinded by the searing light, Saul was taken into Damascus by his companions, where he waited for three days, unable to eat or drink. At the end of this humbling experience, intended to conquer his haughty spirit, Saul received the Holy Spirit and had his sight restored by the Lord, working through a believer named Ananias. Several days later, after regaining his strength, Saul, who now assumed the name Paul, began preaching the story of Christ in the synagogues. Later, he went to Arabia for two years, where God revealed to him the wonderful truths of the scriptures, which he would proclaim as the first true missionary.

Dramatic proof that God is no respecter of persons and that his grace is truly for ALL who believe in Him, was given to Simon Peter in a vision. The story, in the tenth chapter of Acts, tells of Peter going up on the roof to pray one day while visiting in the home of a friend in the City of Joppa. Falling into a trance, Peter saw a large sheet descending from Heaven, filled with all kinds of ..."beasts, creeping things, birds and other creatures."

Upon being instructed to kill and eat the creatures, he replied that he did not eat unclean things, a reference to the old Jewish law concerning diet. The vision was repeated three times and later, as Peter was pondering its meaning, he was told by the Spirit to accompany three servants to the home of Cornelius, a gentile, and to doubt nothing. Arriving at Cornelius' home in Caesarea, Peter reminded his host that it was unlawful for a Jew to associate with gentiles and questioned his motive in sending for him. It was then that Cornelius revealed how God had instructed him to send for Peter, to which Peter replied, "Of a truth, I perceive that God is no respecter of persons; but in every nation, he who fears Him and does what is right is welcome to Him."

Shortly afterwards, as Peter was preaching to a mixed group of Jews and gentiles, the Holy Spirit descended upon all who heard him. As Jew and gentile alike began speaking in tongues, the Jewish Christians were astonished that the gentiles present could also receive the Spirit. It was still another divine revelation that God's plan is for gentiles as well as Jews to receive the gospel and through the power of His Holy Spirit, to become members of His church.

Such vivid examples of God working through His Holy Spirit are generally believed to have been His way of establishing the New Testament Church and dramatically revealing the concept of grace through faith, encompassing all believers as opposed to the Judaic concept of grace only for a relatively small group of people, the Jews.

Today, almost two thousand years later, there are countless examples of the power of Jesus Christ at work in the lives of individuals through the indwelling of the Holy Spirit. Since Christianity involves a direct relationship between an individual and God, aided and directed by the indwelling of His Holy Spirit, few, if any, of the world's more than one billion professing Christians have had identical conversion experiences. Neither have most of them experienced the leadership and power of the Holy Spirit to the exact same degree following their conversion. In the Book of Romans, chapter eight, we are told that the Holy Spirit liberates believers from sin, dwells in them, gives life to their mortal bodies, provides leadership, bears witness that believers are children of God, helps overcome weakness and temptation, intercedes and helps them pray, and secures their eternal salvation. These profiles of individuals from varied ethnic and cultural backgrounds are witness to the fact that grace through faith and the power of the "Holy Spirit" are available to all. And they confirm that the fruit of the Spirit can and does enrich the lives of believers regardless of origin, background or status.

GIFT OF THE SPIRIT

Repent and be baptized and
you shall receive the gift of the Holy Spirit.

Acts 2:38

GOD HAS SPOKEN

God has spoken to the Ages
Through His inerrant word
To His faithful remnant sages
He has spoken, they have heard

He told of man's long journey
Through many centuries past
And how man is always learning
From missteps until at last

Mired in his primeval forest
God reached down from above
To give man grace and solace
Through His son's unerring love

He gave us vital lessons
For living with less strife
Revealing through His son
That we can have eternal life

Then He sent a Holy Comforter
Who dwells within a believer's heart
His Holy Spirit forever after
Giving all who believe a fresh start

Raul A. Gonzalez

Raul A. Gonzalez's
Spiritual Journey

❦

Chapter One

Raul Gonzalez held his hands high for the audience to see. "Look at these gnarled fingers," he implored. "They are the result of many seasons spent harvesting crops as a migrant farm worker during my childhood and young adult years," Gonzalez explained. "I know what it means to work."

Rather than hiding his crooked fingers, Gonzalez proudly displayed them as a badge of honor, an indelible sign of his humble origin. Indeed, Gonzalez had risen from his beginnings as one of five children in a proud family of modest means in Weslaco, Texas, near the Mexican border, to become the first Hispanic ever elected to statewide office in Texas. And he was campaigning to retain his seat on the Texas Supreme Court.

The audience was a statewide group of Texas business leaders assembled in Temple, Texas. The year was 1994. And Gonzalez was being challenged from the left in his own

Democratic Party. Some in the party, unhappy with Gonzalez's judicial decisions and the Supreme Court's shift away from a far left orientation, had generated opposition for him in the Democratic primary. The opponent was a candidate with a well-known family name and strong financial support.

It was a hard fought, expensive, high stakes campaign during which the opposition would use every issue imaginable against Gonzalez, even including television commercials featuring other Hispanic elected officials. The opposition also attempted to use growing secular support for abortion as a weapon against Gonzalez's pro-life position based on his spiritual convictions.

The outcome of the primary campaign was so uncertain that Republicans, who were unlikely to oppose Gonzalez, fielded a candidate in the primary election. In the event Gonzalez won the primary against long odds, the Republican candidate could withdraw, leaving Gonzalez unopposed in the general election.

Following his decisive primary win and withdrawal of the Republican candidate from the general election, Gonzalez would help make political history in Texas with a conservative sweep of legislative seats as well as statewide offices, including George W. Bush's upset of incumbent Ann Richards in the race for governor. He even won on his opponent's home turf.

It was a campaign, which would make both political and judicial history in Texas. But more importantly, it was an experience, which would strengthen Gonzalez's strong spiritual convictions. In retrospect, Gonzalez views the campaign as a classic example of why principle is more important than political expediency in seeking public office.

"I was very gratified at the broad support for myself and for principled candidates for the court," he recalled. "But, I was not proud to have been a part of a campaign in which judicial politics in Texas reached a new low," he added. "I went into the campaign with the commitment to be true to myself and my principles. If I won or if I lost, I was ready to accept God's will," he explained.

The fact that Gonzalez's campaign would receive unprecedented endorsement from the voters in a hard fought primary election, was perhaps also an affirmation of Gonzalez's surrender of his own will to that of a higher authority. In his speech in Temple, and in other campaign appearances across Texas in 1994, Gonzalez gave repeated testimony to his commitment to the leadership of the Holy Spirit, wherever and however that leadership might lead.

It was that commitment to spiritual faith and a search for God's will for his life, rather than money, power and possessions, that had shaped his personal identity, his family and his professional life.

While he had been elected to a full six-year term on the Texas Supreme Court in 1994, Gonzalez retired at the end of 1998, after serving four years of his term and after 14 years on the state's highest court. It was the culmination of some 20 years of public service, including his election as a district judge in Cameron County, his appointment by Republican Gov. William P. Clements to the Thirteenth Court of Appeals in Corpus Christi and appointment by Democratic Gov. Mark White to his initial term on the Supreme Court in 1984.

In a tribute to Gonzalez upon his retirement, fellow Supreme Court Justice Nathan Hecht referred to Gonzalez's first election to the Supreme Court in 1986, after a five-man primary race, a runoff, and a contested general election against a candidate who two years before had come close to defeating a former chief justice. "For that achievement alone, fought hard for and won fairly, pioneering the way for others to follow, Raul Gonzalez will long be remembered," Justice Hecht stated.

But to Gonzalez, judicial politics and election to high

office would merely be one phase of a lifelong spiritual journey and a deep personal commitment to follow the leadership of the Holy Spirit.

Chapter Two

Raul A. Gonzalez comes from sturdy stock. His mother, Paula, and father, Raul, reared their five children in modest circumstances, but in a spiritually oriented home in Weslaco, Texas, near Brownsville, on the U.S.-Mexico border.

One of Gonzalez's most vivid memories is a home altar, which his mother created and which was a focus of her daily prayer life. "She created a shrine with a crucifix and candle and she always had fresh flowers," Gonzalez recalls. "And she would pray daily, not in an organized way, but she set an example for the entire family," he explained.

It was his mother's spiritual life and example, which would sustain her son later in life when he experienced a crisis of faith as a student at the University of Texas.

And it was this commitment to strong personal values, which would help motivate Gonzalez's siblings as well. His sisters, Anadelia and Magdalena, and his brothers, Rene and Hernan, all became first-generation college graduates. Rene followed Raul's example of judicial service, becoming a judge in Anchorage, Alaska. Anadelia was a registered nurse in Corpus Christi before her retirement. Hernan retired from the Brownsville Diocese as a social worker and is pursuing a second career running an antiques business in Weslaco. And Magdalena is an import specialist for the U.S. Customs

Service. Despite its close ties and spiritual focus, life was not easy for the Gonzalez family. Gonzalez's father, who died in 2002 at the age of 89, recruited and transported migrant farm workers, who followed seasonal crop harvests from California and Washington to Arkansas. And Raul's memories of working in the fields alongside his father, maternal grandfather, the late Federico Hernandez, and other family members were a strong motivation to break the cycle and seek a more meaningful and rewarding career.

Life in the fields of Texas' Rio Grande Valley, as well as in states such as Arkansas, California and Washington, meant long hours of hard, backbreaking effort. Work would begin before sunrise and continue until dark, often 15 to 18 hours. Wages were based on piecework so that the quantity of the harvest determined the amount of the pay.

Gonzalez worked a variety of jobs. He would harvest apples in Washington, apricots in California, tomatoes, onions and carrots in Texas, and cotton in Arkansas. Sometimes he would work in the packing sheds, making boxes, which would protect the fruits and vegetables during shipment. Many days his clothes would be green with tomato stains. At times his hands would be swollen after long hours of continuous work. He also spent many hours loading insecticides onto aircraft used to dust cotton and other crops. The lasting physical effects of this kind of labor, both as a child and later as a teen-ager earning money for college, were the gnarled fingers which Gonzalez would proudly display during campaigns for public office in later life.

But, perhaps the most significant effect of this work experience would be the motivation and self-reliance, which would ultimately shape his career objectives and his spiritual life. "I was motivated to succeed by this experience," Gonzalez recalled. "I knew I didn't want to do this for the rest of my life." Another lesson Gonzalez learned was the importance of doing a good job, and that performance matters.

Chapter Three

❧

As a youngster growing up in Weslaco, Gonzalez never considered himself or his family to be poor. While the family's income was modest by today's standards, their home was comfortable and there was always food and other basic necessities. There was also a spirit of sharing among family members and neighbors, a quality, which helped shape Gonzalez's caring attitude toward others.

However, his background, coupled with his experiences in the migrant worker camps and his family's spiritual orientation helped convince him a better quality of life could be his if he was willing to work for it. And the future would demonstrate that he was, indeed, willing to work.

Raul A. Gonzalez has always worked. While in the seventh grade, he started shining shoes in a shoe repair shop. On Saturdays, he helped the nuns clean the Catholic Church where his family worshiped. And it was a spiritual sense of serenity in between these work sessions, when he would sit alone in this place of worship, which helped develop his spiritual identity.

His work alongside other family members in the fields, harvesting seasonal crops as a youth and later, as a young man eager to earn money for college, helped develop his work ethic. He had a good role model. His father was always working. Whether at home or traveling with groups of migrant workers to seasonal harvests, the elder Gonzalez provided a real life example of the virtue of honest, hard work. This served Raul well as he entered The University of Texas at Austin, where he earned a Bachelor of Arts degree in government and later, a law degree from the University of Houston School of Law. Eventually, he earned a Master of Law Degree from the University of Virginia. His academic achievements were made possible not only by his labors as a migrant farm worker, but also by waiting tables, working in the university library and by living frugally in university cooperative housing. These work experiences provided a foundation for his success in private law practice in Brownsville, Texas following graduation, as well as his success in elective office, which required not only long work hours, but days, weeks and months of exhaustive campaigning, as well.

During his fourteen-year tenure on the Texas Supreme Court, Gonzalez earned a reputation for hard work and for his prolific writing. But more importantly, he became known for his fierce independence and objectivity, a character trait shaped by his lifelong commitment to work and the self-assurance that work provides for those who are willing to master it.

Chapter Four

Gonzalez's spiritual growth began with his baptism as an infant. He was confirmed at the age of ten in the Catholic Church, where he became an altar server. Regular attendance at church services, participation in church-sponsored youth activities and enrollment as a student in parochial school, were all strong reinforcements of the spiritual atmosphere at home, exemplified by mother Paula's devout example and her daily prayer and devotionals before her home altar.

As a youth, Gonzalez developed strong respect for the church as an institution and for spiritual truths, such as the Biblical admonition to preserve sexual purity until marriage. (I Corinthians 7:1-9). Then came his matriculation to the University of Texas' main campus in Austin. It was the first time Gonzalez had been away from both family and home, completely on his own.

As a part of his intellectual development and his emerging independence as an adult, Gonzalez began to question his religious faith. As is the case with so many college and university students, he began asking himself questions. Who is God? Is the Bible truly God's word? What do I really believe about God and eternal salvation? His questioning evolved into an attitude of skepticism and Gonzalez began to convince himself that religious convictions were really a matter of individual interpretation. Whatever an individual wanted to believe about God was acceptable so long at it conformed to society's moral standards.

Gonzalez desperately wanted a dramatic religious experience such as that of the Apostle Paul, who was temporarily blinded by God while walking the road to Damascus. This experience would transform Saul of Tarsus, a radical persecutor of Christians, into Paul, a zealous evangelist for Christ, who would become one of the key figures in the Holy Bible and early Christendom. But, as is usually the case with most who make a profession of faith in Jesus Christ as their Lord and Savior, such an experience never came. Rather, spiritual development and growth in faith would be an evolving process, the result of prayer, study, worship and openness to the leadership of the Holy Spirit.

In the meantime, following his secular focus, Gonzalez's participation in worship and church activities became more social than spiritual. His attention and energies became more directed toward social activities and social issues, such as racial equality. And he became less and less focused on worship and personal spiritual growth. This humanistic bent continued throughout his years as a university student and the beginning of his professional career. His focus on career objectives was driven by the desire to be successful by secular standards and a breadwinner for his wife, Dora, to whom he was married in 1963, while in his first year in law school.

Chapter Five

Gonzalez met Dora Champion while they were in the
fourth grade at Saint Joan of Arc Catholic School in
Weslaco. They became friends, as well as classmates. It was
a platonic relationship at first. It was not until three years
after graduation from high school that their courtship began.

Even after their marriage, Gonzalez continued to be
lukewarm about spiritual matters and church attendance in
contrast to Dora's devout religious convictions and loyalty
to the church. Even so, their home was blissful and they
would become the parents of four children. The oldest,
Celeste, lives in Angleton where she works for the Texas
Department of Corrections. Their oldest son, Jaime, works
for a foreign-currency exchange company in Washington,
D.C. and another son, Marco, works for a bank in Dallas.
Their youngest daughter, Sonia, is a full-time mother and
homemaker in Austin. Gonzalez's preoccupation with secular matters and providing for his family and Dora's focus on
their children and the church evolved into a routine existence with little excitement or enthusiasm. By his own
admission, Gonzalez was a prisoner of his own success,
working long hours and leaving little time and energy for
Dora, their children or the church.

It was not until ten years into their marriage that Gonzalez
would be led to a decision that would change his life, his

marriage and his relationship with his children and the church. It was a decision that would enable him to begin growing spiritually. The decision was the result of Dora's suggestion that they attend a marriage encounter weekend retreat. Her religious convictions and her yearning to improve their communication as a couple were reinforced by friends who had attended similar retreats. But like many husbands, Gonzalez resisted. He was comfortable in his role as a successful professional and as a faithful husband, father and family breadwinner. But, after repeated pleading by Dora, Raul agreed to accompany her. Dora immediately made reservations, but when the date arrived, Raul cancelled. Important business matters couldn't wait, even for a weekend. Dora made reservations a second time and again, Raul came up with another reason why it was still not convenient or timely to attend. But on the third time, he had run out of plausible excuses. And they attended what Raul now describes as "one of the best experiences of my life."

That was some 30 years ago, and Raul and Dora are still attending marriage encounter retreats. But, now they attend as speakers and program leaders. They participate in at least two retreats each year and have traveled extensively, to Bolivia, Brazil and Mexico, as well as throughout the United States, to help start similar programs.

Gonzalez recalls the program from that first retreat. It began with an "I" phase, followed by a "We" phase. Then came a "God" phase, followed by a "World" phase. By Sunday morning, Gonzalez remembers that the scales had been removed from his eyes, a Biblical reference to healing miracles, which restored sight. (Matthew 11:5) By then, he had a new awareness of beauty, and a greater appreciation for Dora and their family as he experienced a new love for God through love for Dora. "It was," Gonzalez declared, "a spiritual transformation."

Perhaps it was finally the Damascus Road experience

Gonzalez had been seeking for so long. The marriage encounter retreats are sponsored by Worldwide Marriage Encounter, an organization dedicated to fostering improved marriage relationships in the United States and around the world.

Chapter Six

❦

Now, marital bliss and spiritual growth are daily priorities for Raul and Dora. He often rises at 6 a.m. and tries to spend at least an hour in prayer, meditation and Bible study everyday. Following his retirement from the Supreme Court, Gonzalez joined the Austin office of the Locke, Liddell and Sapp law firm. There he handles a variety of cases, usually involving appeals and arbitration, which draw on his experience of more than 30 years as a practicing attorney, prosecuting attorney and at several levels of the judiciary, including 14 years on Texas' highest court.

But even with a full work schedule, Gonzalez's first priorities are the time he spends each day in prayer and meditation and in his courtship with Dora. They have a standing date every Wednesday at noon. Usually they attend a noon mass at their church, after which they enjoy a relaxed lunch together. There is no regular agenda for their lunch dates. Sometimes they go to a favorite restaurant. At other times they may have a picnic in a park. These dates underscore not only their commitment to each other, but also provide time for sharing their innermost thoughts and feelings with each other. They regularly take walks around the neighborhood together, flirting and smooching like teenage sweethearts. Gonzalez describes their relationship now as "a perpetual courtship."

Church attendance is also high on their list of priorities. Raul believes, and Dora agrees, that the sharing and fellowship with others in Bible study and seeking spiritual guidance is vital for all who seek to lead spiritually directed lives. But, worship and spiritual growth for Raul and Dora does not end with the Sunday benediction. One morning each week, Gonzalez shares breakfast with several friends, during which they exchange experiences and strengthen each other's spiritual resolve. It is what he calls his "accountability" group since they reveal their temptations as well as their spiritual victories. In addition, Gonzalez has begun fasting one day each week. Fasting has a Biblical foundation and Gonzalez finds that such restraint is an important part of personal commitment to a spiritual power greater than self. (I Corinthians 9:24-27).

Raul and Dora also believe that spiritual faith should be manifested through action. Thus, they participate in a hospital ministry, serving the spiritual needs of those with physical disabilities. He also serves as volunteer tutor where he has tried to help underachievers become achievers. Serving as role models for other couples and for young people seeking direction and purpose for their lives is another way in which they attempt to translate their faith into works. "Social action and helping others is not an option," Gonzalez declared. "Rather, it is a commandment from God." (I Corinthians 10:24).

Chapter Seven

Gonzalez's commitment to spiritual growth and service to others grew out of adversity. His struggles as a migrant farm worker, as a student working his way through college and as a young adult seeking spiritual identity all had a leavening affect upon his character and his approach to life. In the migrant worker camps he witnessed up close the toll on human dignity, which results from alcoholism and other forms of personal degradation. These experiences gave him the resolve not to repeat those mistakes in his own life.

As a youngster he recalls the mentoring and support he received from so many individuals such as the late Dr. Armando Cuellar, who served as his scoutmaster in Weslaco. Dr. Cuellar's willingness to take time from his medical practice to minister to young people in his community made an indelible impression upon the young Gonzalez. Even after he enrolled in college, Gonzalez would sometimes visit with Dr. Cuellar when he returned home for a weekend. Dr. Cuellar always encouraged him and they remained friends until his death.

At the University of Texas, Gonzalez recalls it was a librarian who gave him a job, which enabled him to stay in school. And it was another librarian, this one at the University of Houston Law School, who guaranteed a loan, which paid for his and Dora's wedding.

Later, as a young attorney, Gonzalez was inspired by the spiritual example of Federal District Judge Reynaldo Garza in whose court he worked as a prosecutor. "I have enjoyed a lot of help along the way," Gonzalez explained. In gratitude, he added, "My success has come on the shoulders of a lot of kind people."

Out of the hardships, struggles and doubts, Gonzalez has developed some firm convictions about faith in God and about life in general. A cornerstone of his faith is a firm belief in the inerrancy of the Holy Scriptures and their importance as a manual for living. Another foundation stone is the importance of living a "disciplined life." "Discipline is the fruit of the spirit," he explained, underscoring the importance he places on prayer, meditation and study. "Anyone who wants to lead a spirit filled life must be disciplined," he declared.

Gonzalez also stresses the importance of a positive self-image and a positive outlook, refusing to live with guilt, whatever its origin. He cites the Biblical admonition not to be anxious, (Phil. 4;6), pointing out that when a person frets, he is not relying on the presence of God in the person of the Holy Spirit. After all, the indwelling of the Holy Spirit in the hearts of believers is one of the great promises and rewards of the Christian faith, he feels. An unwavering belief in the sanctity of human life—from the womb to the tomb—is another of Gonzalez's strong convictions. "I grieve for America because of the abortion issue, and particularly for those agencies which fund abortions," he declared.

Out of all of these experiences has come a conviction that the civil justice system can and should be a healer and a peacemaker, rehabilitating individuals rather than simply punishing them. This explains Gonzalez's growing interest in mediation and the importance of resolving disputes short of litigation.

Thus, he has developed a perspective of the judicial system and of government at all levels as less and less important as arbiters of social problems. "The real solutions to society's problems are not to be found in Austin or Washington," Gonzalez stated. "Instead, they can be found through the teaching of values because real change must occur within the heart," he explained. "This means our public schools should be teaching civic virtues," he added.

Chapter Eight

A s featured speaker at a Texas Prayer Breakfast on February 25, 1999, Gonzalez outlined his views on the importance of living a "balanced life." "We rarely take time out to look at the important questions in life because we are too busy," he explained. Jesus gave us guidance in establishing proper priorities in our lives, he said, citing Matthew 22:37. In response to a question, Jesus said. "You shall love the Lord your God with all your heart, with all your soul and with all your mind. This is the greatest and the first commandment. But in Matthew 22:39, Jesus added a second priority. He said 'You should love your neighbor as yourself.' The whole law and the prophets depend on these two commandments." Then Gonzalez cited I John 4:20, which states, "If anyone says 'I love God,' but hates his brother, he is a liar; for whomever does not love a brother whom he has seen, cannot love God whom he has not seen. Whoever loves God must also love his brother." In conclusion, Gonzalez said life's most important priorities are the individual's relationship with God and with others and that they are inseparable.

Gonzalez's spiritual journey, reinforced by his experiences as a youngster growing up in a family of limited means, and his professional perspective as a practicing attorney and lower court judge, inevitably shaped his decisions as a justice on the Texas Supreme Court. In an essay for a "Faith and The

Law Symposium" at Texas Tech University, later published
by the Texas Tech Law Review in 1996, then Justice Gonzalez
declared, "There are some who believe that religious beliefs
should be private and have no bearing on their work. There
are others, like myself, who believe that we are called to live
our faith full time, not just on Sundays, and that all our
thoughts, words, and deeds should be impacted by our religious convictions. To me, it is an inescapable fact that our perspective on any issue is influenced by where we place
ourselves on the religious spectrum. To deny this fact is to be
dishonest." Then, disclaiming any pretense at being a "model
Christian" Justice Gonzalez wrote "I make no judgments
about anyone. I merely observe the obvious—that there are
differences in levels of commitment to religious beliefs and
that these differences do influence our decisions."

Several Supreme Court decisions cited in the essay illustrate this point. One was Nelson v. Krusen, 678 S.W.2d 918
(Tex.1984). It was his first opinion as a Supreme Court justice and his first controversial case. Mrs. Nelson and her
husband had a child with Duchenne muscular dystrophy.
They did not want another child with the disease. When she
became pregnant again, she consulted Dr. Krusen to deter-
mine whether she was a genetic carrier of the disease. Based
on test results, Dr. Krusen assured her that she was not a carrier and the Nelsons decided not to abort their unborn child.
Approximately three years after the birth of the child, it
became evident for the first time that he did, in fact, have
muscular dystrophy. The Nelsons brought suit against
Dr.Krusen on their own behalf for "wrongful birth" and for
negligent failure to properly advise them and also brought
suit on behalf of their minor son for "wrongful life." The
Nelsons also brought suit against Baylor Medical Center for
negligent testing procedures.

The trial court granted summary judgment for the defen-
dants on the basis that the two-year statute of limitations

barred the Nelsons' claims. Further, the trial court stated that no cause of action for "wrongful life" exists in Texas. The court of appeals affirmed the lower court decision. However, the Supreme Court reversed the judgment of the court of appeals as to the statute of limitations. The limitations period of the malpractice act arguably began running at the date of the last examination by Dr.Krusen and, if applied literally, it would have barred the Nelsons' cause of action before they knew it existed. The Supreme Court held that the limitations provision of the malpractice act was unconstitutional to the extent it purported to cut off an injured person's right to sue before the person had a reasonable opportunity to discover the wrong and bring suit. Thus, because there was not time within the statute of limitations when the son's condition could have been discovered, the Nelsons' cause of action for "wrongful birth" was not barred by limitations. This cause of action had been approved by a prior case and the court did not reconsider its prior approval.

The high court also noted that the child's cause of action for "wrongful life" was not the same as the parents' cause of action for "wrongful birth." To sustain his cause of action, the child must assert that his cause arose as a result of his birth and that his damages are based on the fact that he is alive. Stating that the judicial system is not in a position of being able to assess life (even impaired) as opposed to no life, the court held that no such cause of action exists in Texas.

Justice Gonzalez wrote both a concurring and a dissenting opinion. He agreed with the court on the statute of limitations issue, but disagreed with the court's disposition of the other issues. He further wrote that neither the Nelsons nor their minor child should have a cause of action for either "wrongful birth" or "wrongful life." He joined another justice in calling for overruling of the prior case, which had affirmed such a cause of action. In outlining his opinion, he wrote, "This case presents some very difficult questions, both moral and legal. When courts are forced to contend with issues involving life and death such as those presented in this case, a merger of our concepts of morality and law is unavoidable.

"Since the United States Supreme Court's decision in Roe v. Wade, we have witnessed a tremendous increase in the number of abortions in this country, all in the name of 'free choice' of the 'right of privacy.' Under this social policy, a parent or parents of a child are free to abort their child during the first trimester of pregnancy for any or no reason. This policy has contributed to a 'disposable society.' If we do not like something, we get rid of it. Often, in abortions, this is done without regard for the sanctity of life. It is my hope that the courts and legislatures of this nation, and our society, will continue to ponder the meaning and value of life, even that of those yet unborn. Through this process of reflection and discussion, hopefully the pendulum of public opinion will swing toward the recognition of the rights of the unborn."

Writing such a morally focused opinion in the mid-80s required great courage because of the overwhelming secular support for abortion rights. Justice Gonzalez's opinion was vilified by many and it was an issue used against him in all of his subsequent re-election campaigns.

Justice Gonzalez stood alone in another case involving a question of whether a person's word should be his bond. In Kennedy v. Hyde, 682 S.W.2d 525 (Tex.1984) the issue was whether an oral settlement agreement was enforceable in light of the Texas Rule of Procedure 11. One of the parties to an agreement changed his mind and refused to honor the agreement. The case was tried before a jury and the jury held against the party trying to escape the agreement. The court of appeals affirmed. A majority of the Supreme Court reversed and remanded the case for a new trial on the basis that the oral agreement was not in compliance with Rule 11. Justice Gonzalez disagreed with the court that the agreement was in dispute. He wrote, "It was clear to me that the only dispute was that one of the parties to the agreement had changed his mind and chose not to be bound by the agreement. My faith teaches me that unless there are extenuating circumstances, such as fraud or misrepresentation, people ought to live up to their commitments." He further stated that, "it used to be that a man's word was his bond. I regret that the court's opinion facilitates a further erosion of this value."

In a litigation-driven society, Justice Gonzalez wrote another courageous, dissenting opinion in 1992. It was Cox v. The Evergreen Church, 836 S.W.2d 167. In this case, a member of the church, who was also a member of the administrative board, dropped off her son at the church's daycare center. She slipped and fell on the entranceway, which was slick from rain water. She filed a personal injury action against the church, an unincorporated charitable association. The trial court granted summary judgment for the church and the court of appeals affirmed the decision. However, the Supreme Court abolished the common-law rule that prohibits a member of an unincorporated association from bringing a cause of action for negligence against the association and reversed and remanded the case for trial. Justice Gonzalez opposed abolishment of the doctrine, pointing out that the high court, in effect, was allowing the plaintiff to sue herself.

Chapter Nine

T hese are brief examples of a long litany of cases where Justice Gonzalez acted with independence based upon moral and religious principles, as well as objective interpretation of the law. It was a stance, which was inconsistent with the philosophy of the Texas Supreme Court at the time, but was generally consistent with law and the moral and religious beliefs of a large percentage of Texas residents.

When Gonzalez became the first Hispanic on the Texas Supreme Court in 1984, it was a troubled time for the Court. The Court had developed a reputation in some circles for being a subjective body, prone to making new law, rather then being a body, which could be counted on to objectively interpret the law without regard to the parties involved. The Court would undergo a dramatic change in this regard over the next decade. But, in the meantime, it was hardly a cohesive, collegial body. According to Gonzalez, there were tensions among individual justices due to philosophical differences and personality conflicts. There was a feeling among some of the electorate that the Court was not an impartial arbiter of the law. This resulted in the start of a reform movement at the grassroots.

Thus, the new Justice Gonzalez would play a pivotal role in the transformation of the court over the following decade and beyond. The fact that in the opinion of many, the state's highest court now enjoys positive dynamics, with mutual trust and confidence among most of the justices, is a source of great satisfaction to the now retired justice.

Another source of satisfaction has come from seeing many of his court opinions ultimately validated, even though they may have been unpopular or in the minority at the time. It's another reinforcement of Gonzalez's strong belief in principle over political expediency.

Now in his early sixties, with his family grown and educated, and with a distinguished record of public service as a judge and the first Hispanic to serve on the Texas Supreme Court, what does the future hold for Raul Gonzalez? He declares a lack of any firm agenda or personal goals at this time. "I want to be obedient to God and open to the leadership of the Holy Spirit," he explained. "I like what I'm doing," Gonzalez said of his current career as a practicing attorney.

But remaining open to new opportunities for service to God and his fellowman will be central to his and Dora's future. "I hope to have many years of productive life and I want those years to be obedient to God," he declared.

KEEP MY COMMANDMENTS

If you love Me, you will keep my
commandments. And I will ask the
Father and He will give you another Helper,
that He may be with you forever; that
is the Spirit of truth, whom the world
cannot receive, because it does not
behold Him or know Him, but you
know Him because He abides with you
and will be in you.

John 14:15-17

A LITTLE VOICE

I thought I heard a little voice
A whisper in my ear
It could be only a chance noise
A soft breeze far or near

On the other hand it may have been
A song bird's mating call
Nature's symphony now and then
With a message of peace to all

But, I rather think it was God's own voice
Speaking softly and clearly
Declaring His will is my own choice
Because He paid for our sins so dearly.

Don G. Kaspar

Don G. Kaspar's Spiritual Journey

꧁꧂

Chapter One

W hen 26 year-old Jacob Kaspar stepped off a ship at the Port of Galveston in 1868, he was uncertain about what to expect. The recent graduate of Chrischona Seminary in his native Berne, Switzerland was simply following the Biblical admonition to carry the gospel message of Jesus Christ to the ends of the earth.

And as he viewed his new mission field, a mosquito infested swampland that was Southeast Texas, he may have thought at times that he had come to the end of the earth. He had completed a trans-Atlantic journey of almost two months. He was thousands of miles from the comfort of his family and the familiar surroundings of his native Switzerland. And he was alone. But he felt a spiritual call to minister and to teach on this rough and tumble frontier in a promising part of the New World.

It was a frontier plagued by the aftermath of the war between the U.S. and Mexico, and Civil War reconstruction. It was fraught with hardship stemming from natural disasters and other vagaries of frontier life.

And it was at an early stage of Texas statehood, established in 1845 after Gen. Sam Houston had won independence for Texas in 1836 by defeating the Mexican army, under Gen. Antonio Lopez De Santa Anna, at the battle of San Jacinto, only a few miles up the coast from Galveston.

But, according to a story recounted in "A History of The Kaspar Family," written by the late Edgar Herbert Kaspar, the youthful minister was undaunted in pursuit of his mission. In accordance with prior arrangements, he boarded a train in Galveston for a short trip southwestward along the Texas coastal plain toward Freyburg, in Fayette County. Upon arriving in Freyburg, he was met by a parishioner in an "ochsenwagen," an ox-drawn wagon with a mule tied at the rear. After their greeting, the parishioner untied the mule and instructed the young minister to ride to the home of his host. When the minister asked for directions, the parishioner replied, "der esel weist den weg." Translated, this meant, "the mule knows the way."

The mule did, indeed, know the way. Following a short ride, the animal stopped in front of a farmhouse where children were playing in the yard. "Do you know this mule?" he asked the children. "Yes, that is our esel," they replied. "Then, I am home," Kaspar declared, as he climbed down from the animal's back.

Thus, began a preaching and teaching ministry, which would continue until his retirement at the end of the Nineteenth Century. And it would mark the beginning of a Kaspar family business and spiritual legacy, which would eventually span five generations, with more to come.

Don G. Kaspar, great grandson and fourth generation descendant of Jacob Kaspar, is the central figure in this story. As president of Kaspar Wire Works in Shiner, Texas, a short drive from where great grandfather Jacob would begin his ministry, Kaspar has expanded the scope of the family's influence, while remaining true to its high calling. He presides over a family-owned business which has helped changed the face of the Texas economy, and indeed, that of the nation. At the same time, he has remained close to his spiritual roots, exhibiting a sense of personal humility, a calling of service to others and a loyalty to his family that honors the legacy of his great grandfather, his grandfather, August and his father, Arthur. These are the same qualities which motivate his sons, David, Dan, Doug and Dennis, who continue the family tradition as his business partners.

It is interesting to note the similarity of the name, Shiner, Texas, where Kaspar Wire Works is located and where the Kaspar family lives, and the name, Shinar, as recorded in the tenth chapter of Genesis. Shinar was the location of the first kingdom established by Noah's great grandson, Nimrod, following the great flood, which God used to punish mankind and start civilization anew some sixteen centuries following the banishment of Adam and Eve from the garden He had given them near Eden. Shinar literally means the land of two rivers, the Tigris and Euphrates. However, Shiner, Texas, named for the late Henry B. Shiner, and also located between two Rivers, the Guadalupe and Colorado, in South Central Texas, stands in stark contrast to the Shinar of the Old Testament, which was the cradle of the Babylonian Empire, noted for its disobedience to God. Shiner, Texas is a community of hard working, God fearing people whose churches and lifestyle are symbols of obedience.

Don Kaspar's story, and that of the Kaspar family, is not about making money or achieving personal recognition. Rather, it is about a spiritual journey which began with a young Swiss immigrant missionary more than a century and a third ago, and which has continued generation after generation. It is a living example of how spiritual qualities such as faith in God, and a commitment to basic virtues, such as honesty and respect for others, can be exalted in a secular environment even as it is exalted from the pulpit.

Don Kaspar doesn't think of his role as that of a minister. His personal humility and his unpretentious lifestyle won't permit it. But, as he walks through his plant calling his employees by their first names, as he mingles with business contacts throughout the nation, and as he quietly provides both the financial support and personal leadership for community service organizations, including his church, he is following the path that his great grandfather, Jacob, charted for the family four generations ago. Indeed, he is following the leadership of the Holy Spirit in all that he does.

Kaspar demonstrated this spiritual commitment even in his formative years, as a student at Texas A&M University, a time when so many youngsters are prone to rebel against spiritual values which they have been taught at home. Attending both Sunday School classes and worship services at Northgate Methodist Church, near the campus, Kaspar noted that few other students were in attendance. He and a fellow student decided to do something to remedy the situation. They went to the registrar's office and obtained some 800 names of fellow students who had noted a similar religious preference on their admission records.

Obtaining permission from the CQ, the charge of quarters who monitored required study periods and conduct of cadets, Kaspar and his friend used the time to visit students in their rooms, delivering information about church activities and issuing a brief oral invitation to attend. They made over 100 visits the first week. The following Sunday, so many cadets responded that they overflowed the seats and sat on the floor. By the third week more than 100 were in attendance and a second class was formed to accommodate the overflow.

Charles Glass of Beaumont, Texas, a retired electric utility executive, who was Kaspar's roommate for two years at A&M, and who has remained a close friend for more than a half century, attests to Kaspar's spiritual qualities from a unique perspective. He was best man in Don and Jean Kaspar's wedding and they regularly hunt and fish together, visit in each other's homes and share other activities with mutual friends.

"Don demonstrates a genuine personal humility in both his personal and business relationships, which understates his commitment to deep spiritual values," Glass observed. "He has a mischievous sense of humor which also masks his spirituality," Glass stated. "But the fact that he doesn't wear his religion on his sleeve and doesn't force it on others makes his witness even more compelling," Glass explained. "Don has a good heart and a spiritual quality which are reflected in his relationships with everyone he meets," Glass added.

Chapter Two

❧

While the Rev. Jacob Kaspar had intended that his ministry be carried on from one generation to the next, he could hardly have imagined the eventual impact his legacy would have from both a spiritual and economic point of view.

Jacob had been licensed to preach as a Lutheran minister in 1869 and had been ordained in 1870, in the Black Jack Parish, in South Central Texas. Initially he preached and taught school in the homes of settlers, most of whom were German immigrants who shared similar cultural and language backgrounds. His first pastorate was at the Salem Church at Freyburg. The Salem congregation would become affiliated with the Lutheran Church, Missouri Synod in 1876. It was while he was preaching and teaching at the Salem Church that he met and married Marie Elizabeth Platke of White Oak, a settlement about nine miles west of what today is downtown Houston. His bride had immigrated to Texas with her family in 1852 from her native Bredin, in East Prussia, Germany.

Jacob and Marie would become the parents of eleven children, the oldest of whom was August, born in 1871, while the family lived in Freyburg. And it was through August that the family would begin a multi-generation tradition of service by creating individual economic opportunity based on honest work, integrity and respect for others.

Believing that August was called to the ministry, his parents enrolled him in a Lutheran seminary in St. Louis. And while he did not complete his seminary training, August learned to play the organ and developed a spiritual orientation, which led him into service as church organist and choir director as a layman in later years.

Despite his religious background and his spiritual training, August was destined to find his place of service in a more practical way. He liked the outdoors and he liked to work with his hands. So, at the age of 19, August struck out on his own, migrating to the small Lavaca County hamlet of Shiner. His father had moved the family from Salem Church to Ebenezer Church on the San Antonio prairie, near Lincoln in 1877 and to St. John Church at Cypress in 1889, at about the time August left home. While at Ebenezer, the family had lived under the same roof with the church and school, where Jacob taught as well as preached.

In the Shiner area, August first worked as a cowboy on the Fred Kokernot Ranch. Hard work and a frugal lifestyle enabled him to eventually buy 100 acres of land, three miles west of Shiner, for $3,000. It was here that he would begin farming and eventually establish a family business, Kaspar Wire Works, which, a century later, would become known, both nationally and internationally, for quality service, as well as quality products. As Lavaca County's largest employer, Kaspar Wire Works, at the close of the Twentieth Century, provided stable jobs and good benefits for hundreds of residents from Lavaca and surrounding counties. And at the start of the Twenty-First Century, the future looked even more promising than the past.

Chapter Three

❦

Despite its status today as an innovative manufacturer, committed to the well being of its employees, as well as its customers, Kaspar Wire Works had an humble beginning, built on the free economic principle of finding a need and filling it.

The need which August Kaspar saw was very real and practical. As a farmer, he found that corn shucks were messy and could create problems unless they were contained. So, he began crafting wire baskets by hand to contain the shucks until they could be fed to farm animals or disposed of otherwise. Perhaps it was fate that barbed wire had by this time replaced smooth wire as the preferred material for fencing. Thus, an unlimited supply of smooth wire was now available, with much of it being discarded as useless. So, when he was not laboring in the fields, August began making baskets, not only for containing corn shucks, but also for gathering farm produce. Using hand tools, such as pliers, he laboriously crafted the baskets using the discarded wire.

One day a neighbor saw one of the baskets and asked whether he could buy one for himself. August sold him one of the baskets for a dollar. Thus, a business was born. As August made additional baskets in excess of his own needs, he began selling them throughout the area from the bed of his wagon. A short time later, he saw an opportunity to sell his baskets through merchants rather then from his wagon. So, by 1902, he was a manufacturer and he had a way to distribute his products.

Then, another market developed. Farmers in the area were experiencing a problem in preventing their "dumb esels" from eating their row crops while plowing. August's experience making wire baskets and his entrepreneurial drive inspired him to begin crafting mule muzzles from the same discarded wire. At a price of 15 cents each, muzzles began selling faster than August could make them. In his limited "spare time," he was crafting each one individually using a pair of hand pliers.

Thus, faced with the dilemma of making baskets and muzzles or farming for a living, August chose the former. Selling his farm, August bought a two-acre tract in Shiner and by 1904 was engaged fulltime in manufacturing wire products in a small shed in his backyard. It was here that Kaspar Wire Works was born.

Soon, the fledgling company was manufacturing and selling baskets and muzzles throughout Texas. Another development, the construction of the San Antonio and Aransas Pass Railway, provided a convenient, economical channel for getting the products to expanded markets. As demand increased, August's creative business instinct took over. He began using a gasoline engine connected to overhead drive belts for straightening and cutting wire. And he invented his own tool, similar to a ratchet screwdriver, to simplify the task of gripping and twisting wire to the desired shape. In 1908, he was granted patent #906634 for his wire basket design. However, it was not enforceable because he missed the two-year time limitation for applying for the patent. At the beginning of a new millennium, the original wire basket design was still in limited production by a long-time employee. It has stood the test of time and a changing economy, with practical as well as antique value.

While business flourished over the next 25 years, the demand for feed baskets and muzzles declined as farming became more mechanized. Tractors replaced horses and mules in the fields, reducing demand for muzzles. And the advent of ground and mixed feeds, along with baling of hay, further reduced the need for baskets. The firm's last order for muzzles was shipped in April, 1949. It was for 120 dozen muzzles from Shapleigh Hardware Company in St. Louis. And it marked the end of a product line, which had helped sustain the company for almost half a century.

August was joined in the business by his eldest son, Arthur, who had graduated from high school in 1918, as World War I was coming to a close. Arthur was the only one of August and Emma Kaspar's seven children who demonstrated an interest in the family business. His knack for business and his enthusiasm were instrumental in the company's transition into new product lines. The first products added were florist easels and wire wreath frames. While they were still manufactured using crude hand tools, they marked the beginning of an important diversification. Soon thereafter, the small company was manufacturing wire coat hangers.

Around 1920, welded wire products began appearing on the American market and as electric power came to Shiner, electric motors began replacing gasoline engines as a primary source of energy. Kaspar Wire Works purchased its first electric motor in 1921, a one horsepower, single phase, 110 volt Westinghouse model, which cost $115.

The company's first electric spot welder was purchased in 1928, the year in which Don Kaspar was born, enabling the company to enter the welded wire products market. The first products were welded wire clothes baskets used by gymnasiums and swimming pools. They are still sold today to high schools and colleges throughout the country. Also in 1928, the company purchased its first typewriter, made by Oliver. It cost $48, postage paid. August had started the business working 16 hour days. Ten hours were spent in the shop and another six were spent keeping books, writing letters and handling other administrative chores. Thus, the addition of a typewriter was an important step in reducing the length of the workday, as well as helping handle more business. August's wife, Emma, and Arthur's wife, Josephine, whom he married in 1927, worked alongside their husbands in paying bills, writing invoices and letters and doing other administrative chores necessary for the business to succeed.

Despite rumblings about the onset of the great depression, the company bought property bordering a new highway being constructed north of town, and built a 40x100 foot building. It had completely outgrown the backyard shed in which it had been founded. The fledgling company did well through the year 1931. But the following three years were difficult. In 1933, at the height of the depression, sales for the year totaled $6,725.44. By working 12 hours per day, six days each week, and with no help except in the plant, Arthur was able to keep the company operating. He later recalled that the line of wire products for floral shops was primarily responsible for the company's survival since people continued to spend money for funerals even when they had money for nothing else.

Expansion of the highway system in surrounding states, as well as Texas, provided another market for diversification and expansion with production of wire supports for steel reinforcing bars used in constructing concrete roadways. And Kaspar Wire Works played a key role in the 1930s in developing a new product, which would eventually touch every consumer and every home in America. It was the use of wire shopping baskets in grocery stores, which led to the use of shopping carts as grocery stores evolved into supermarkets. The first order for shopping baskets went to ABC Stores in Houston and by 1937 shopping baskets accounted for 45 percent of the company's sales. It was that same year that production of shopping carts began. Weingarten Market in Houston bought the first order of carts and Handy Andy Stores in San Antonio placed the second order. Thus, a national trend was started, which not only made shopping easier for the consumer, but also enabled grocery stores to move from labor intensive practices of handing items to customers on request, to a self-service concept where food items were displayed in aisles accessible to shoppers. Because of limited aisle and storage space in stores, the company developed a folding double deck cart, also in 1937. Another innovation was a cart with a child's seat made from wood, with a leather safety strap.

Kaspar Wire Works' production of shopping carts attracted national attention and the company received visitors from all over the country. It was something of a phenomenon to have food store executives, manufacturers and others coming to a small Texas town to see firsthand a product innovation which would help change one of the nation's most basic activities, grocery shopping. This phenomenon would be repeated in later years, as newspaper technicians from New York to California would make regular visits to Shiner for training in maintaining another Kaspar innovation, the coin operated newspaper vending machine.

Leather straps for the shopping cart child seats were purchased from another Texas firm, which would also become nationally known. It was the Tex-Tan Company in nearby Yoakum. Tex-Tan, which would later become a part of the Tandy Corporation based in Fort Worth, now Radio Shack, Inc., developed a reputation for its leather products. And its first order for wire display racks for belts was placed with Kaspar Wire Works in 1937. Tex-Tan's chief executive was the late C.C. Welhausen, whose daughter, Jean, would later become Mrs. Don Kaspar.

Chapter Four

❧❧❧

One of the company's most serious challenges was posed by World War II, just as it was experiencing growth, both in size and product diversity. As strategic materials such as steel and wire were diverted to the war mobilization effort, it became increasingly difficult to maintain a satisfactory level of operations. Thus, production almost came to a stop, except for a few orders from the military for frying baskets for mess halls and handles for ammunition boxes. There were also orders for shopping baskets and carts from post exchanges at nearby military installations, such as the U.S. Naval Air Station at Corpus Christi and Fort Sam Houston in San Antonio. Also, the company was able to supply clothes baskets for defense plant locker rooms, similar to baskets it had been manufacturing for use in school gymnasiums. However, the operations dwindled to the point where only two employees remained until the war ended and operations could be resumed. During this difficult period, Arthur Kaspar, who was too old for active military service, served without pay or expense reimbursement as a member of the Lavaca County Rationing Board. As the war effort expanded and as strategic materials became scarcer, this became a demanding, time-consuming service.

With the end of the war and cancellation of restrictions on strategic materials, Kaspar Wire Works began expanding operations again. The fact that the plant and all of its equipment had been maintained just as it was at the start of the war made the startup relatively easy. And the company's good credit rating with suppliers through the years assured prompt shipment of materials.

Potato chip manufacturers rushed in with orders for pyramid floor stands, some as tall as a Christmas tree, for package displays. Other pre-war product lines soon were in full production. And there was even a small flurry of orders for feed baskets and horse muzzles, but volume remained small,

The post-war period provided many opportunities for product diversification. A new fad in ice cream merchandising was "frozen drumsticks." Thus, a market developed for sliding trays on which the cones could be stored and frozen after being filled with ice cream, dipped in chocolate syrup and covered with peanuts, thus creating a drumstick. Over a period of three to four years, the company shipped tens of thousands of these freezer baskets to every major city in America. Display racks also continued in strong demand as manufacturers of various products from cookies to fishing tackle sought the marketing advantage of good visual presentation.

Technological innovation, while an asset, also became a liability for the Kaspar company. The grocery shopping basket and cart revolution, which the firm had pioneered, became a liability as chrome plating became the preferred finish. The Kaspar products had been painted. And lacking chrome plating facilities, or the ability to install them, the company phased out of the cart market. Among its last shipments of green painted nesting carts was an order from a Venezuelan government export-import agency in 1952.

But other product lines, such as wire racks and crates, were expanded and soon the company was manufacturing soft drink bottle racks, commercial refrigerator baskets and even baskets for holding meat being cooked over barbecue grills. And innovation continued with development of a compact cart for holding and transporting supplies and equipment for janitorial services in large office buildings. Thus, the Kaspar "Kleaners' Karry-All" developed into a steady seller.

Perhaps the most important product innovation in the company's history was the coin-operated newspaper vending rack. In 1956, Arthur Kaspar called on the San Antonio Light in an effort to sell them more of the racks then in use. However, the Circulation Department expressed its dissatisfaction with the "honor racks" as they were called, because more than half of the papers were being taken without payment. And while a California firm had developed a coin operated rack, it held only a dozen papers. What The Light and the newspaper industry needed, it was explained, was a secured, coin-operated rack, which would hold at least 100 newspapers.

So, Arthur returned to the plant and immediately called a planning meeting of his top assistants to develop such a product. By this time, Don Kaspar had joined the firm full-time, following his graduation from Texas A&M University in 1949, and a tour of duty as a U.S. Army infantry officer in Korea. Don was Arthur and Josephine Kaspar's only child and he readily joined the company, having worked part-time and summer vacations during his high school and college years. In fact, he had performed odd jobs at the plant since he was twelve years of age.

The result of the planning session was a rack, which displayed a folded newspaper's front page in the door, with a coin mechanism on top, which accepted five cents for the daily paper and 20 cents for a Sunday edition. And it held 100 papers. The Light immediately ordered 50 of the racks at $15 apiece.

Thus, an innovative move by a small Texas company started a revolution in newspaper distribution throughout

America and even in a few areas in Europe. Through Don Kaspar's marketing efforts, the company soon was receiving orders from The New York Times, Washington Post and other large circulation papers throughout the country. Fortunately, the company stopped selling the racks direct at $15 apiece, losing money on each one, and entered into an agreement with an established distributor of newspaper supplies. The result was the nationwide marketing of the Kaspar "Sho-Rack," the copyrighted name which continues on the product line today. And Sho-Racks are regularly exported to other countries such as Germany, Austria, Holland and Switzerland.

Even so, Kaspar Wire Works continues to grow, adapting to a changing business environment and the need to adapt existing products to meet changing requirements or to add new products. But despite some inevitable change and new leadership from a fifth generation of Jacob Kaspar's line, the company continues to focus on its fundamental strengths. These include a priority on quality, supported by highly personal service, delivered by a workforce, which is considered to be part of the family. And while growth is inevitable, the firm is not interested in growth for growth's sake. Rather, growth should be a response to changing customer requirements, according to Kaspar.

The Kaspar success formula is firmly rooted in the character and moral precedent of great grandfather Jacob Kaspar. As Don Kaspar explains it, basic honesty and personal virtue are the most important requirements for joining the Kaspar workforce. "I am a real believer in looking at moral character first," he declared. Only after applicants have met this requirement are they evaluated for their physical and mental aptitudes.

This approach enables the company to develop its own managers, as well as train its own craftsmen and craftswomen. "We have trained every employee, from welders and press operators to jig builders and die makers," Kaspar stated proudly. And he takes pride in pointing out how small town and rural people make such fine craftsmen because they are both intelligent and conscientious. What he modestly fails to point out is the pride he takes in being able to provide the economic opportunity through which his employees can achieve individual dignity and a good quality of life.

Another key aspect of the Kaspar success formula is fiscal responsibility. This means living within its means, paying its bills promptly, providing for its employees and investing retained earnings in the business rather than diverting them to other uses.

Because of its conscientious attention to details and solving problems promptly, the company has earned loyalty from its employees, as well as its customers. There are no unanswered grievances and there has never been an effort to unionize the workforce because, Kaspar pointed out, there is an atmosphere of "mutual respect" between management and employees. The company provides liberal paid holiday and vacation benefits and pays for one-half of health insurance costs for employees and families. In keeping with the company's philosophy of individual fiscal responsibility, Kaspar insists that every employee should be responsible for a portion of his or her healthcare. This also helps curb any tendencies toward over utilization and thus, contains overall costs. There is also a profit sharing plan, as well as a trust to provide retirement benefits for eligible employees.

The company contributed liberally to a local hospital foundation in order to assure delivery of healthcare services to employees and their families and for the community. Despite this local support, the hospital failed as a result of what Kaspar feels was unsound public policy. It also encourages staff leadership in community service organizations, providing administrative support such as photocopying and secretarial assistance.

Summarizing his philosophy, Kaspar said, "When it comes to business, two plus two still equals four. Everybody has to make a profit and everybody has to give good service. If you don't give good service and don't make a profit, you can't stay in business."

Chapter Five

D on Kaspar and Jean Welhausen were married following his tour of duty with the U.S. Army in Korea.
Jean had graduated from the University of Texas where she
majored in mathematics. Having grown up in Yoakum, only
a few miles from Shiner, she and Don happily adapted to
small town life in Shiner. He was busy growing the family
business and active in community and church activities. She
was active in community, church and arts organizations, as
well as the Texas Exes, the University of Texas alumni organization. Later, she would serve as national president of the
alumni group and during her term, she and Don would
embark on a worldwide tour, visiting chapters in 10 coun-
tries, including cities such as Hong Kong, Tokyo, Cairo,
New Delhi, Bangkok, Athens and Paris.

The Kaspars built their dream house, a rambling, contemporary style residence in Shiner, where they reared their
four sons and where they still live. Friends and family who
enjoy the Kaspars' generous hospitality are treated to a cor-
nucopia of wild life trophies and personal memorabilia,
which exemplify their laid-back lifestyle and love of nature.
A trophy elk, which Don bagged on their ranch in the moun-
tains of Northern New Mexico, at one time almost covered
the fireplace, with its rack nearly touching the floor. Don
shot the elk near dusk one evening and had to walk several

miles back to the ranch house to get help and a truck to transport the carcass. He and a hunting companion field dressed the animal, carrying each quarter section several hundred yards to the truck. It was midnight by the time they got back to the cabin, almost frozen and totally exhausted. The story of this feat has become a part of the Kaspar folklore, enjoyed by friends and family alike.

Both Don and Jean are avid wildlife enthusiasts and conservationists, making frequent visits to their ranch properties in Texas, as well as New Mexico, to assure that wildlife and nature maintain a proper balance. They approach hunting as a way to preserve this balance and to promote quality of both habitat and herd. In addition, they selectively support breeding and production of beef cattle on their ranch properties.

They are never happier than when bouncing over rough ranch terrain in a four-wheel drive vehicle, binoculars in hand to get a close-up view of the harmony of nature. And they delight in sharing the experience with friends who are invariably awed by what they see and feel.

Attired in jeans, open collar, western boots and hat, Don is equally at home on the range or in his office in Shiner. While he wears a suit and tie on more formal occasions, he is rarely without his boots and hat. Jean is equally at home in ranch attire or sophisticated high fashion. But, both are as down-to-earth as the people next door. Reluctant to flaunt their success and good fortune, they are more prone to share it with others. Jean is the sponsor of numerous scholarships for deserving students at the University of Texas. Both her generosity and her leadership resulted in her being named a "Distinguished Alumnus," the University's highest recognition for its graduates. She has also served as a member of the Texas Historical Commission by gubernatorial appointment.

Jean's commitment to historical preservation led her to restore a building just off Shiner's main street, which she named "The Peachtree." The building serves as a repository for antiques as well as a meeting place and community social center.

Jean has also contributed to Shiner's cultural life as a benefactor of the historic Gaslight Theater, where she regularly acts in, as well as directs live stage productions. Don is equally generous. He is the recipient of the Boy Scouts of America Silver Beaver award, which recognizes outstanding volunteer service on the council level. He has served in various capacities, including cub scoutmaster, scoutmaster, troop committee chair and council board member. And Kaspar Wire Works has provided most of the funding for purchase and maintenance of the Boy Scout troop facility in Shiner. One of Don's more important state leadership positions was serving a term as state chairman of Texas Association of Business & Chambers of Commerce, which represents Texas employers on public policy issues in both Austin and Washington, D.C.

Don and Jean are parents of four sons and doting grandparents of 10. Following in their father's footsteps, all four sons graduated from Texas A&M University. Jean, the Texas Ex, is equally proud of this achievement though she feigns dismay as a way of keeping the family's male contingent humble. As proof, she was an active member of the Lavaca County Texas A&M Mothers' Club and is a past president of the State Federation of Texas A&M Mothers' Clubs.

Also following the example of their father, grandfather and great grandfather, all four sons have become partners in the family business. Each is responsible for a division and profit center for the company. David, the eldest, graduated with a business administration degree in 1975 and has responsibility for Sho-Rack sales and refurbishing. Dan graduated in 1977 with a degree in agricultural economics and handles administrative matters for all divisions. Douglas received a degree in industrial engineering in 1980 and handles engineering and environmental matters, as well as the electro-plating operations and Kaselco, a new electro-coagulation environmental product. Dennis graduated in 1984 with a major in mechanized agriculture and is responsible for family ranch lands in addition to wire products and a new "Ranch Hand" product line including bumpers for ranch vehicles.

All four sons not only followed their father at Texas A&M, and into the family business, they also share his modesty and his approach to life and business. Like their father, all four earned the rank of Eagle Scout. And all share their parents' love of nature.

Chapter Six

D on Kaspar's spiritual journey began as a child. His mother, Josephine, and his father, Arthur, set a moral tone in their home and their personal lives which shaped his spiritual development. Kaspar recalls that he never heard either his parents or any of his grandparents utter a profane word. In keeping with this high personal standard, the family was devout in its participation in and support of the church. "I was expected to attend Sunday School and church services regularly. I thought that was what everyone did," Kaspar explained.

Josephine Kaspar had been a faithful member of the Methodist Church in Yoakum, Texas, where she grew up. Arthur Kaspar had been a Lutheran, following the example of his father and grandfather. The Lutheran Church in Shiner was very small and was visited once each month by a circuit-riding minister who also served other small churches in the area. Arthur Kaspar played a pump organ for the services, which occasionally were conducted in German as a courtesy to the church elders who were of German ancestry.

A controversy developed, however, when the minister decided he would not conduct funeral services for anyone who was not a member of the church, even for close relatives of loyal members. This decision was too harsh and fundamentalist for Arthur. Thus, he moved his membership to the

Methodist Church. Don never perceived this move as being disloyal to his Lutheran heritage or to his great grandfather's legacy as a Lutheran missionary on the Texas frontier. Rather, the family adopted a more ecumenical approach to their own spiritual lives and to the community. As an example, Don's father sang tenor and his grandfather sang bass in a double quartet, which regularly performed at funeral services without regard to the deceased's religious orientation. They considered this part of their religious, as well as civic duty. And while Don didn't follow their example as performing vocalists, as a young man he recalls teaching himself to sing by accompanying vocalists on his car radio.

Don's maternal grandmother, Susie May, descended from a family which declared itself "good Catholics" and thus, qualified for a Mexican land grant near Yoakum. Later, she married a Methodist, R.E. McMaster. Their children later became members of Catholic, Methodist and Baptist churches.

As a teenager, Don Kaspar made a profession of faith and joined the First United Methodist Church of Shiner, which he has continued to serve in a variety of capacities over the years. These include 12 years as chairman of the administrative board, chairman of the building committee, during which time a new sanctuary was built, and chairman of the endowment fund, a position he currently holds.

At age 16, Kaspar entered Texas Agricultural & Mechanical College, then an all-male, military, technical institution, where he spent four years as a member of the Corps of Cadets. This experience strengthened him spiritually because it developed his ability to relate to others, honed his organizational and leadership skills, and taught him a degree of self-discipline.

Graduating just prior to his twentieth birthday with a bachelor's degree in agricultural administration and a commission in the U.S. Army Reserve, he would have to wait until age 21 to report for active military duty. Kaspar spent the next 14 months working at the family business until he was ordered to report for active duty.

Chapter Seven

A commonly held view in some circles is that military service has a detrimental effect upon many youngsters because it exposes them to individuals and influences which are alien to them. On the contrary, Kaspar is convinced that young women and men joining the military tend to associate with those who share their own interests and values.

Thus, he found it was unnecessary to become involved in degrading activities such as using profanity, gambling, and drinking alcoholic beverages in order to be both accepted and respected. In retrospect, Kaspar observed that those who were drawn into such degrading pursuits usually lost the respect of their comrades and diminished their ability to become leaders. He is firmly convinced the same principles apply in business or any other activity today.

Second Lieutenant Kaspar reported to the U.S. Army Fifth Regimental Combat Team in Korea on Christmas Day, 1951. He felt secure since he was reporting for combat duty after most of the heavy fighting had subsided. Even so, there were frequent skirmishes and general harassment back and forth between U.S. and North Korean forces. He recalls frequent shelling by the enemy and numerous injuries to companions from exploding shell fragments, as well as a close call himself.

The day Kaspar reported to battalion headquarters, three miles behind the front lines, there seemed to be a general malaise among the troops. This was readily apparent by observing several fellow officers who were nursing hangovers from a raucous Christmas party the night before. It was also apparent that the unit lacked necessary supplies and discipline. Kaspar was assigned to share a wooden floor tent with two other officers. He was assigned to a cot whose previous occupant had been relieved from frontline duty due to mental stress. The previous occupant's rifle and personal effects were still in place and overhead there was a bullet hole in the tent. As he sat alone eating lunch, he recalls overhearing two senor officers lamenting about having too many World War 11 veterans who had been recalled to active duty from the reserves. What they needed, both agreed, was more fresh "A&M trained" officers. Thus, Kaspar saw a challenge and he readily accepted it, without ever acknowledging that he had overheard their conversation.

Over the next several weeks, conditions improved as the unit was re-supplied and morale was raised through training and discipline. A member of Kaspar's platoon, a carpenter in civilian life, had become a troublemaker and a bad example for others in the unit. Learning of the soldier's occupational skills, Kaspar assigned him to build a badly needed washstand for his tent, using discarded wooden crates. The washstand proved to be so well built and useful, the man was assigned to build one for every tent in the unit. Upon receiving appropriate recognition and attention for his work, the soldier soon became a positive rather than a negative influence in the unit. This was an important lesson in human psychology, which would serve Kaspar well throughout his active duty tour and in his subsequent business career. Also, there were combat experiences in Korea, which strengthened Kaspar's spiritual faith.

One day, his company was deployed over a hill and

across a valley as it approached the main line of resistance. The troops were spread over a large area to avoid attracting enemy fire. However, a group of South Korean laborers, employed by the army, suddenly appeared, drawing fire from the North Koreans. When one of the laborers was hit in the arm by a shell fragment, Kaspar bandaged the gaping wound, splinted it using his bayonet and scabbard and helped him back to his group. On another occasion, Kaspar's compassion for others appeared to be a factor in his own survival.

Recently promoted to the rank of first lieutenant and serving as assistant battalion operations officer, Kaspar, along with two non-commissioned officers, was scouting a "blocking" position which could be used by a reserve group in the event the enemy were to break through the main line of resistance. After identifying the position, Kaspar was guiding officers from each of the battalion's three companies through a well-used combat zone so they would be familiar with it in the event they needed to use it. Walking along a trail, one of the group tripped over a wire, igniting a "Bouncing Betty" bomb.

The bomb was so named because after a small explosion at ground level, it would shoot about 20 feet into the air where a larger explosion would occur, projecting shrapnel in every direction. Diving to the ground at the sound of the first explosion, Kaspar thought he had avoided being hit. Then he felt a liquid running down his right hip and leg. Examining himself with his hand, he discovered he had been hit in the canteen, which was hanging from his belt. The canteen and cup had been so mangled they could not be separated. He had escaped serious injury, and possibly death, by mere inches. One of the non-commissioned officers had been hit in the chest, sustaining minor injuries. Hiking more than a mile back to his jeep, Kaspar discovered for the first time in his life just how thankful he was to be thirsty.

On another occasion while still in Korea, Kaspar had a

spiritual experience on a snow-covered mountaintop, under a full moon. A non-commissioned officer had stopped by his bunker to notify him of an officers' meeting at the company commander's bunker at 8 p.m. As he hiked along a trail, enroute to the meeting, he stopped momentarily to take in the stark beauty of the rugged landscape, punctuated by tree stumps, which had been sheared by heavy artillery barrages. As he sat on a rock for a moment surveying the scene, he was reminded of the words to the song, "Hark The Herald Angels Sing," particularly the phrase, "God and sinners reconciled." Kaspar was struck then by the truth that as a sinner, reconciled with God through faith in Jesus Christ, that he had a mission for his life and that he would be spared from injury or death during the remainder of his combat service. "It was clear that I must serve Him," Kaspar recalled. Arriving at the command bunker a few minutes later, he was advised that there must have been some miscommunication. No meeting had been called that night.

Chapter Eight

J ean Kaspar's spiritual journey, like Don's, was greatly influenced by her family. A strong woman herself, she recalls that all of the women in her family were strong, especially in a spiritual sense. Her great grandmother, Liza Welhausen, started the first Sunday school at the Methodist Church in Shiner. And to make certain children attended, she would hitch up her horse and buggy so that she could pick them up and then take them home after services. Her grandmother, Henrietta Welhausen, and her mother, Mary Elizabeth Welhausen, were also strong Christian witnesses. Her mother taught Sunday school, played the piano and provided generous financial support to keep her small Christian Church in Yoakum open. "She was the spiritual leader of the family," Jean recalled. Jean's great grandfather, Charles Welhausen, served as a captain in the Confederate Army, later becoming a state legislator, merchant and banker.

Following the spiritual legacy of her forebears, Jean has supported Don in providing strong spiritual leadership for her family and church. She has taught Sunday school, led youth groups and served in a number of special capacities. One example is the living nativity scene which she has organized and directed for the church and the community for many Christmas seasons. Involving a cast of some 100, Jean explained that the production is "our gift to Shiner."

As a child, Jean was baptized and joined the Christian Church in Yoakum, where her family attended. She joined the Methodist Church in Shiner after her marriage to Don. Her childhood spiritual experience made her aware of the importance of rearing their four sons in a spiritual atmosphere. Honesty and trust were a major element in her relationship with her sons, along with a willingness to talk with, listen to and counsel each one individually and privately. As a result, there was never any need to demand compliance with family standards of conduct.

This philosophy has extended to youngsters beyond her immediate family. At any given time, Jean is sponsoring some 20 scholarships for deserving students at Texas A&M and the University of Texas. Over the years, her generosity and faith in action has enabled more than 100 young men and women to attend one of these universities. It is a contribution which is paying huge dividends to society and which, Jean said, renews her faith in the future.

Don believes that he and Jean, who observed their fiftieth wedding anniversary in 2002, have had "a wonderful marriage and fulfilled life" because of their love and consideration for each other and their spiritual values. "Building a business and rearing four sons presented no problems we could not overcome because of these values," he explained.

HIS SPIRIT
INDWELLS YOU

But if the Spirit of Him who raised
Jesus from the dead dwells in you,
He who raised Christ Jesus from the
dead will also give life to your mortal bodies
through His Spirit who indwells you.

Romans 8:11

THE HOLY COMFORTER

Jesus sent a Holy Comforter
To dwell within our hearts
In His absence to defer
And cause sin to depart

Through faith in Him
There is love and grace
In our hearts a hymn
Giving life a new face

It is a gift of grace to all
From life's chafe to flee
Through His Spirit walking tall
Toward believers' eternal destiny

Rev. Bertram E. Bobb

Rev. Bertram E. Bobb's Spiritual Journey

~~~

Chapter One

Riding along the winding road from Antlers to Tuskahoma, Oklahoma, historic home of the Choctaw Nation of Oklahoma, the Rev. Bertram Bobb, in an act of worship, suddenly burst into song from the rear seat of the car. The chaplain for both the Choctaw Nation of Oklahoma and the Inter-Tribal Council of the Five Civilized Tribes was singing number 48 from a book of Choctaw hymns in a strong, melodic voice, which belied his almost 80 years of age and declining eyesight.

From memory he chanted the lyrics of the Choctaw hymn. It is a prayer to the Holy Spirit for comfort and guidance in overcoming the hardships of the Choctaw during troubled times such as the "Trail of Tears," the forced march in the 1830s of many Native American tribes from their ancestral homelands to designated Indian territory west of the Mississippi River. Rev. Bobb pointed out that the hymn might be doctrinally questionable since it intones the Holy Spirit to descend from Heaven to comfort them rather than acknowledging His indwelling in the hearts and minds of believers in Jesus Christ. But it is, nevertheless, evidence of the sincere faith of some of his people in Christ as their Savior and in fulfillment of His promise to send a Holy Comforter to indwell His faithful, filling the void created following His resurrection from the tomb and ascension into Heaven, Rev. Bobb explained.

The Choctaw language uses the English alphabet, although only 17 individual letters are used, rather than the alphabet's entire 26 letters. There are no sounds for the letters C, D, G, J, Q, R, V, X and Z in Choctaw, although there is a sound for the letters C and H combined, or CH. There are also replacement sounds for the other omitted letters according to the Choctaw Nation Language Department. The Choctaw language is also phonetic in its spelling and pronunciation. Thus, some Choctaw words are understandable. For example, Jesus in Choctaw is spelled "Chisus." Since there is no sound for V, the Hebrew word Jehovah in Choctaw is Chihowa, which has a similar sound. Many words are not as discernable. The text of Hymn 48 in Choctaw, entitled "Prayer To The Holy Spirit," is as follows:

Shilombish Holitopa ma!
Ish minti pulla cha,
Hatak ilbvsha pia ha
Ish pi yukpalashke.

Pi chukvsh nusi atukma
Ant ish okchvlashke,
Ish pi yohbiechikbano;
E chim aiahnishke.

Shilombish Holitopa ma!
Pim anukfila hvt
Okhlilit kvnia hoka
Ish pi on tomashke.

Pi chukvsh nukhaklo yoka
Ant pi hopohlvchi :
Il aiashvcheka yoka
Ish pi kashoffashke.

The literal English translation is as follows:

Shilombish—Spirit or Ghost
Holitopa—Holy, Sacred
Ma—Personal Salutation, Acknowledgment

Ish—You
Minti—To Come
Pulla—Certainly, Surely

Hatak—Man or Mankind
Ilbusha—Poor, Wretched, Low, Meager
Pia—We, Us
Ha—Definite Article Showing Which One

Ish—You
Pi—For Us
Yukpa—Rejoice, To Cheer
Lashke—Will

Pi—Our, We, Us
Chukush—Heart
Nusi—To Sleep, Slumber
Atokma—Recent Past Tense

Ant—Come
Ish—You
Okchulaske—Will Wake

Ish—You
Pi—We, Us, Our
Yohbiechikbano, Yohbiechi—To Make Mild, Sanctify
Bano—Wholly

E—We
Chim—Your
Aiahnishke-Aiahni—To Wish
Ishke—A Particle Used As An Intensitive Having The Force
   of the English Word
"Do."

Shilombish—Spirit of Ghost
Holitopa—Holy
Ma-O, Thou—Personal Acknowledgment

Pim—Our
Anukfila—Minds
Hut—Definite Article Showing Which One

Okhlilit—Darkness
Kunia—Leaving or Going Away
Hoka—Sign of Past Tense

Ish—You
Pi—Us
On—Upon
Tomashke—Will Shine

Pi—Our
Chukush—Hearts
Nukhaklo—Sorrow
Yoka—Past Tense Expression

Ant—Come
Pi—Us
Hopohluchi—To Comfort

Il—We
Aiashucheka—Sin or Mistake
Yoka—Past Tense Expression

Ish—You
Pi—For Us
Kashoffashke—Will Clear

The English paraphrase of the hymn is as follows:

Come, O Holy Spirit!
Come to us who are poor in spirit.
Bless us!

Come and awaken our hearts.
Give us your peace,
We implore you.

O Holy Spirit!
Our minds are clothed in darkness.
Enlighten us!

Our hearts are filled with sorrow
Come and comfort us,
Sinners that we are.
Cleanse us!

This and other hymns provided great comfort to the Choctaw as they endured the long journey from their ancestral homeland in Mississippi to what is now Southeast Oklahoma. They would march, rest and sing, as they endured hunger, fatigue, exposure to adverse weather conditions and other hardships. Thousands of men, women and children perished during the months-long ordeal, which occurred in stages over a period of several years. The Trail of Tears is one of the painful chapters in the history of Native Americans, the result of the Indian Removal Act passed by the U.S. Congress and implemented by President Andrew Jackson. When negotiations for their removal to the West failed, President Jackson used military force to implement the law, promising food, transportation and necessary support for the trip. Instead, the Choctaw and members of other tribes were forced to walk much of the distance, enduring broken promises, extreme privation and death for many.

From the rear seat, Rev. Bobb sang other Choctaw hymns, illustrating the influence, which early missionaries had on Choctaw culture and their continued impact centuries later. One of the hymns is entitled "Christ Bled For Me," number 47 in the Choctaw Hymn Book.

According to a paper entitled "Old Choctaw Beliefs," written by Jesse Ben, the Choctaw have always believed in a creator. They believed He watched them through a hole in the sky, the sun, during the day and through another hole in the sky, the moon, at night. And in "An Introduction To The Choctaw Language," Todd Downing suggests the Choctaw were receptive to early Christian missionaries who arrived around 1817, inviting them into their nation to help establish churches and schools.

It is obvious that Rev. Bobb enjoys singing hymns, something he does well and often. Most Choctaw enjoy singing gospel songs, he explained, even though only a small percentage of them are true believers in Christ. He is regularly requested to direct singing of a Choctaw hymn at services of the Antlers Bible Church, where he preaches periodically. As chaplain of the Choctaw Nation of Oklahoma, he also leads worship at major Council meetings and at special events such as groundbreaking ceremonies and building dedications sponsored by the Nation. Moreover, he is present at all events sponsored by the Christian Indian Ministries, Inc., (CIM) of which he is founder and president. Christian Indian Ministries, Inc., is the culmination of a ministry serving God and Rev. Bobb's native people, spanning more than four decades. It is a ministry at which he continues to work vigorously in spite of his age and declining health. CIM is located at P.O. Box 9, Antlers, Ok., 74523.

Chapter Two

Bertram E. Bobb was born March 30, 1924 in Smithville, Ok., located in McCurtain County, in the southeast corner of the state. His father was the Rev. Johnson Wilson Bobb, a Methodist minister. His mother was born Mary Estell Edwards, for whom he was given his middle name. Later, he dropped the "s" to make it Edward rather than Edwards. Both were full blood Choctaw.

Thus, Rev. Bobb grew up in a Christian home where he acquired the spiritual foundation, which would ultimately lead him into the ministry. He recalled attending Sunday School and church services regularly. Since there was no Christian literature in the Choctaw language at that time, his teachers relied heavily upon memory work in his native language. Church attendance was reinforced by prayer and devotional time in the home. Prayers were regularly said at bedtime and there were prayers of thanksgiving before meals, coupled with Bible study and devotionals. Spiritual matters were a topic of discussion around the family dinner table.

His father had been orphaned at an early age, growing up in the home of relatives. Rev. Bobb has no written genealogical record of his father's youth or his conversion experience. But, it is obvious he was given spiritual guidance, learning strong character traits as a youngster. For example, he avoided using either alcohol or tobacco in contrast to many of his peers. Rev. Bobb recalled that as a member of the U.S. Army's 37th Division during World War I, his father assumed a spiritual leadership role among his fellow soldiers. He would serve as counselor and mentor to many of his younger and less mature comrades. His father, who died in 1943, is a namesake for the Johnson W. Bobb-Kennedy Myers United Methodist Church, founded in 1948. It later became the District Center for the Southeast Oklahoma Mission Conference, comprised of a number of other Methodist Churches within the district. The Rev. Johnson W. Bobb served as pastor of a number of other Methodist churches, ultimately becoming a district presiding elder in the Methodist Church.

Bertram Bobb had three siblings. Two sisters died in infancy. A third, Evangeline Bobb Wilson, lives in Chickasha, Ok. She is a professional educator. Her husband, Victor W. Wilson, is retired from the Bureau of Indian Affairs and is of the Cherokee-Delaware Tribe.

Mrs. Wilson helped organize the Choctaw Code Talkers Association, an organization whose mission is to preserve and commemorate the heroism demonstrated by a group of Choctaw military veterans. During World War I this group of Choctaw soldiers was called into action when all previously coded communications of a military nature, relayed by U.S. and Allied forces, were decoded by the enemy and crucial battles were being lost as a result. The Choctaw soldiers coded key military terminology into the Choctaw language and transmitted undecipherable messages, which helped achieve major victories, resulting in a victorious and early conclusion to the war itself. Information pertaining to this highly classified top-secret military operation was not declassified until 1968. Three members of this group were close relatives of Rev. Bobb and many of the group entered the gospel ministry following their military service

Chapter Three

❦

B ertram Bobb began his formal schooling at the age of nine in the Schults Public School at Haworth, in the extreme southeast corner of Oklahoma. He was delayed in starting to school because Indian children were neither required, nor encouraged to attend school at that time. And schools were not always readily available.

After one year, he transferred to the Jones Male Academy, a government sponsored school in Hartshorne, Ok., where he spent the next three years. Then, he attended the public school in Hugo for a year before transferring to the Goodland Presbyterian Orphanage School. Though he was not an orphan, he was extended the privilege of attending the school because his father was its first graduate. There he completed the tenth grade before volunteering for military service during World War II. On Nov. 11, 1942, Rev. Bobb's father signed papers permitting his son to volunteer for service in the U.S. Navy at age 18. He did so within a matter of days. "Three years, two hours and 15 minutes later," Rev. Bobb recalled, he was discharged. It was on Nov. 18, 1945. During his active duty service, Rev. Bobb was a signalman at the Ford Island Naval Station at Pearl Harbor, Hawaii. One event he remembers vividly was the raising of the Battleship Arizona, which was sunk by Japanese bombs on Dec. 7, 1941. The site is now a memorial to those who lost their lives that day.

Following his discharge from the Navy, Rev. Bobb earned his high school diploma by completing requirements for the General Equivalency Diploma (GED). He then enrolled in Murray State College at Tishomingo, where he completed a two-year program in arts and sciences. He excelled in football and boxing as extracurricular activities. Since he had a natural aptitude for numbers, he also completed 36 credit hours in accounting while in residence at the Chillicothe Business College in Chillicothe, Mo. Later, he completed requirements for a Bachelor of Science degree in accounting, with a minor in business education, at Northeastern State University in Tahlequah, Ok.

Rev. Bobb married Mary Ann Greenwood, a childhood classmate from Goodland Presbyterian Orphanage School, in 1950. Mrs. Bobb, also of Choctaw heritage, was born and reared in Antlers, attending a one- room school there before transferring to the Goodland Presbyterian School, where she met her future husband. Bertram Bobb and Mary Ann Greenwood were simply classmates and friends during their years at Goodland. It was only after his return from military service during World War II that they would begin a courtship. Their courtship was strengthened through their participation in a group led by Rev. Bobb's mother, who was volunteer director of youth activities for their church.

Mrs. Bobb, who died in November, 2002, always stood by her husband and supported his ministry in many ways over the years. For 15 years she directed food services and functioned as chief cook for the Bertram Bobb Bible Camp (BBBC). She was well-known for her down-home Southern style of cooking and for her expertise in preparing traditional Choctaw dishes such as "banaha," also known as shuck bread, and "holthponi," a dish consisting of shredded pork and hominy and, of course, fry bread, a native specialty.

Rev. and Mrs. Bobb reared three sons. Johnson Wilson Bobb II, namesake of his paternal grandfather, is a jeweler for a company in Soper, Ok. Wesley Edwin Bobb lives in Gallup, New Mexico, where he is on the staff of the Native Bible Fellowship Church. And Frederick Bertram Bobb lives in Antlers where he assists his father in administering the Christian Indian Ministries program of work. They have two grandchildren, Deborah Estell Bobb and Bertram E. Bobb II. Their father is Johnson Wilson Bobb II.

After graduation from Northeastern State University, Rev. Bobb moved to Tulsa to begin what he anticipated would be a long career as a professional accountant in the private sector. But, after working several years, first for an electronics firm, and later for a smelting and refining company, he realized something was missing in his life. While he enjoyed working with numbers, he lacked a sense of joy and fulfillment. Something was missing.

Rev. Bobb had made a profession of faith in Jesus Christ and had become a member of the Methodist Church at the age of 10. It was not a dramatic conversion such as that experienced by the Apostle Paul on the Damascus Road. Rather, it was a decision made after thoughtful consideration and counseling with his minister father. Rev. Bobb had become spiritually aware before the age of 10, but had been advised by his father and church leaders to wait until he was more mature to make a formal profession of faith. Growing up in the church, he recognized that most Christian Indian churches are oriented toward adults, not youth. So, he learned by observing his elders, but without the benefit of literature in his native language, which would have helped strengthen his spiritual development. His yearning for a more spiritually fulfilled life led him to take a correspondence course on "The Good News of The Gospel" through the Moody Bible Institute (MBI). It would change the course of his life. "Through this course, I began to understand the concept of the Trinity—God the Father, God the Son and God the Holy Spirit—and how the Holy Spirit actually lives within the hearts of believers," Rev.

Bobb explained. Also, at about this time, Rev. Bobb heard a poignant, prophetic sermon by Dr. John Walvoord of Dallas Theological Seminary. Dr. Walvoord was preaching at the Tulsa Bible Church on the eternal plan of God. After hearing this message, Rev. Bobb asked himself how he fit into God's plan and why. A follow-up discussion with Dr. Walvoord inspired Rev. Bobb to seek a deeper spiritually directed plan for his life through an in-depth study of the Bible.

Finally, at the age of 32, married and the father of three sons, he would yield to the leadership of the Holy Spirit, answering God's call to enter the ministry. He was licensed to preach by the Methodist Church in 1956 and began teaching classes in his church, first for junior high students and later for adults. But, he recognized the need to continue his theological training. Thus, with the guidance and help of former mentors, he enrolled in the Dallas Theological Seminary in Dallas, Texas. One of these mentors was Ms. Sammy D. Hogue, who had been his Bible teacher at the Goodland Presbyterian Orphanage School, then working at MBI.

Rev. Bobb temporarily settled his family in Antlers at a country home on family property and moved into dormitory quarters at Dallas Theological Seminary. Working as an accountant for a plant nursery and later for an accounting firm, he was able to send money to support his family. Mrs. Hogue paid the $50 per semester tuition at the seminary. In addition to his work and studies, he began a ministry teaching in the homes of Indian families who had been resettled in Dallas as part of the federal government's ever-changing policy concerning the role of Native Americans in contemporary society.

Some 200 Indian families had been settled in what was called the Elmer Scott Community Project in South Dallas as a result of a law the U.S. Congress enacted in 1953, aimed at relieving the federal government from direct responsibility for Indian affairs. The law effectively allowed the government to unilaterally end protection of land in tribal reservations, transferring responsibility to the states, and encouraging relocation from reservations to urban areas, thus hastening extinction of Native American tribes. The government's policy concerning Native Americans had changed several times prior to 1953 and it would continue to change in subsequent years.

In his book "The Choctaw," part of a series on "Indians of North America," Jesse O. McKee, retired professor and chair of the Department of Geography and Area Development at the University of Southern Mississippi, and Frank W. Porter III, general editor of the series, recount the patchwork of policy changes and inconsistencies by the federal government toward Native Americans over almost two centuries. They recount that beginning in the 1830s with the federal government's coercion of eastern tribes to relinquish ancestral lands and move west of the Mississippi River to designated Indian Territory, its policy has changed numerous times. As recently as 1983, The Reagan Administration restated the unique "government to government" relationship between the United States and Indian nations. Since that time, federal programs have moved toward transferring responsibility for Indian affairs to individual states, which have sought control of Indian land and resources according to McKee's and Porter's works.

In whatever way the government's policy inconsistencies toward Native Americans may be interpreted, they demonstrate that some good can be found in almost any circumstance. Thus, the attempt at homogenizing and urbanizing Native Americans in the 1950s provided a mission field for Rev. Bobb and an important step in development of his Christian ministry to his native people.

Chapter Four

⚜

Among some 200 Indian families resettled in the Elmer Scott Community Project in Dallas were members of several tribes from a number of different locations. In addition to Choctaw, there were Chickasaw, Creek, Cherokee and Seminole, which comprised what came to be known as the Five Civilized Tribes. These were the tribes, which had the earliest exposure to Christianity through the work of early missionaries and to the culture of white settlers. There were representatives of other tribes, as well. Rev. Bobb recalled that he regularly came in contact with representatives of some 70 different tribes during the course of his ministry in Dallas.

Rev. Bobb's teaching was based on the scriptures and how Christianity compares to traditional Native American religions, which often involved nature worship, superstitions and even witchcraft. He also provided counseling on issues related to the families' transition into general society and their search for new occupational skills. He even assisted families with such practical problems as preparing income tax returns. The classes were conducted for small groups in homes at various times convenient to the students.

This demanding regimen continued for about a year, until Rev. Bobb realized that he could not master the challenge of classes in Hebrew and Greek, while working, caring for his family and ministering to his native people, as well. So, after prayerfully re-evaluating his priorities, he left the seminary and helped organize the Dallas Indian Methodist Church as a mission of the United Methodist Church. He was assigned as pastor. He also began attending classes at Dallas Bible College (DBC) as time permitted and served as an accountant for DBC.

Using facilities owned by a sister Methodist Church, Westerfield Methodist Church was chartered in far west Dallas with about 15 Indian families. It grew steadily to include approximately 150 members. Later, the new church would move into its own facilities in a house which Rev. Bobb managed to acquire in the Oak Cliff Section of Dallas. They quickly outgrew this facility, but were able to acquire a larger house in the same area. Ultimately, doctrinal differences would develop because Rev. Bobb's more conservative theology, developed through his classes at Dallas Theological Seminary, sometimes differed with doctrinal views held by some of his denominational sponsors. His use of seminary students to teach classes at the church also rankled some of the sponsors.

These doctrinal differences ultimately led Rev. Bobb to leave the Methodist Church. He then founded a non-denominational Christian Indian Chapel in the Oak Cliff area. It first met in a house and later purchased a small church building. Rev. Bobb worked as an accountant for a nursery and landscaping firm and later for a certified public accounting firm to support his family and enable the Holy Spirit to lead in establishment of his ministry independent of any denominational sponsor.

In conjunction with starting the Christian Indian Chapel, Rev. Bobb helped to establish an independent, non-denominational agency in an effort to reach fellow Native Americans beyond the traditional church setting. Finally, the stress of an urban ministry and the desire to return home to Oklahoma led Rev. Bobb to resign as pastor of the Chapel in 1982 and return to Antlers to focus on working with his native Choctaw people.

Chapter Five

After moving back home to Antlers, a small Southeast Oklahoma town of some 3200, Rev. Bobb organized the Oklahoma Indian Evangelism component of CIM.

Included in the ministry of CIM is a summer camping program for Native American youth from eight to twelve years of age and a program for teens in grades seven through twelve. The youngsters spend Sunday night through Friday at the camp at a tuition cost of $25, a nominal amount, which makes the program accessible to more youngsters. Some scholarships are provided according to need. The weeklong curriculum includes Bible study, music, water and team sports, crafts and recreational activities. Moody Bible Institute students conduct some of the sessions, along with missionaries and staff.

Weekend retreats are also conducted in the spring and fall. All of the camping and retreat activities are conducted on a twenty-five acre campsite owned by the Ministries on Pine Creek Lake at Ringold, Ok., between Antlers and Broken Bow, Ok. An adjoining 35 acres owned by Rev. Bobb personally is available for camp use as needed.

Another ministry of CIM is a weekly radio program, The Christian Indian Broadcast, which has been heard on Dallas station KSKY for some 35 years. It is aimed at a Native American audience. A newspaper published by the

Ministries, The Christian Indian News, ceased publication because of increased demands on Rev. Bobb's time and his declining health.

In addition to leading the work of CIM as president, Rev. Bobb preaches periodically at the Antlers Bible Church, serves as chaplain for the Choctaw Nation of Oklahoma and Inter-Tribal Council of the Five Civilized Tribes, conducts other meetings and services and writes a monthly column for "Bishinik," the official publication of the Choctaw Nation of Oklahoma. In one column, he said "The great need today, whether the Native American Nations or America, is for Christians to learn the secret of daily victory over sin. Too many are burning up energy in struggles within themselves." He was referring to the power of The Holy Spirit in directing the lives of believers in Christ, a power, which he relies on daily in his own life.

The CIM has oversight by a volunteer board of trustees, including business, community and lay leaders. One trustee is a professional forester and business owner, one is an engineer, another is a retired technician and still another is a retired Seminole Indian minister. Rev. Bobb's son, Fred, also serves as a trustee and assists in administering the Ministries' programs.

Operating on a modest budget of approximately $100,000 annually, CIM relies upon personal contributions from individuals who recognize the importance of the mission programs it carries out. Rev. Bobb maintains a modest lifestyle, primarily on income from social security, honorariums he receives for conducting various services and attending meetings of the Choctaw Nation of Oklahoma.

Rev. Bobb's ministry and his zeal for winning others to Christ has had a far- reaching impact, well beyond his native people. Joe L. Hanson, a lay leader in the Trinity Bible Church of Richardson and a trustee of Dallas Theological Seminary, is one of those who has been inspired by Rev.

Bobb's dedication. Hanson and his wife, Betty, were introduced to Rev. Bobb's ministry through the mission program of their church.

Betty Hanson joined other ladies from their church in spending time at the Bertram Bobb Bible Camp, cooking for children attending the camp. Youth from their church would also participate by performing various chores to help open the camp and keep it running smoothly. Hanson recalled that his own youngsters, daughter, Pam, and son, Gary, gained insight from their experience with a culture much different from their own in the affluent Dallas suburb of Richardson. Because of their knowledge of Christ, and despite their lack of material possessions, Hanson pointed out, the Choctaw youth were just as happy as his own youngsters, who enjoyed both.

Hanson said his family has been "significantly impacted" by the ministry of Rev. and Mrs. Bobb and the sacrifices they made, though it was obvious to him that neither Rev. Bobb, nor his late wife, considered their service to be a sacrifice at all.

Chapter Six

An appreciation of the service provided by Rev. Bobb's Christian Indian Ministries organization, and his zeal for ministering to his people is strengthened by studying the history of the Choctaw. According to legend, as recounted by Rev. Bobb and in the book, "The Choctaw," there are different accounts of the origin of the Choctaw. One account concerns two brothers named Chata, sometimes spelled Chahtah, and Chicksah, who parted company over personal differences. Chata founded the Choctaw Tribe and Chicksah founded the Chickasaw Tribe. Moving from the West toward the East, Chata and his people would place a stick in the ground each evening. The next morning they would move in whichever direction the stick was leaning. Finally, one morning the stick was standing upright and a white dog, which had slept at the base of the stick each night, had died. This was interpreted as a sign that they were home. Thus, they settled on fertile, wooded land in South Central Mississippi. There they built a large ceremonial mound where they buried the bones of their deceased. Because the mound leaned, they named it "Nanih Waiya," which is translated literally as "leaning hill." Another legend has the Choctaw emerging from the damp earth of the mound, after being created by a great spirit. According to Prof. McKee's account, it is believed this mound was used for political and religious meetings of the Tribe from about 500

B.C. until the arrival of European settlers in the area in the early 1700s.

Over the centuries, the Choctaw established a stable society, building villages and homes and growing crops, as well as fishing and hunting. With the coming of the white settlers, including some missionaries, they became one of the Five Civilized Tribes. Some Choctaw remain in Mississippi as private citizens today, descendants of those who chose not to relocate to the West in the Indian removal effort by the federal government during the 1830s.

Rev. Bobb's ancestors were among the survivors of the "Trail of Tears" march, which covered more than 2000 miles, much of it on foot, in harsh weather and often with little or no food. They were settled in designated Choctaw territory in what today is Southeast Oklahoma. His great grandfather, Bob Thioltubi, was one of the survivors.

When the Dawes Commission was developing the roll of those with certified Indian blood, it had difficulty spelling his name. Thus, he was listed simply as Bob, which became the surname Bobb. The surname Thioltubi literally means "chase and kill" in Choctaw, according to Rev. Bobb. The Dawes Commission, named for Henry L. Dawes, chairman of a committee appointed by President Grover Cleveland to negotiate the termination of the five civilized tribes' land titles in the 1880s, was charged with compiling a list of those with a Certified Degree of Indian Blood (CDIB) and thus, eligible to receive individual land allotments. The roll was closed in 1906, when Oklahoma became a state and the allotment program was ended in 1907.

Chapter Seven

According to a history of the Choctaw written by Len Green, former editor of the Choctaw newspaper, BISHINIK, the federal government established a three year program for removal of the Choctaw from Mississippi to what is now Southeast Oklahoma. It was decided that about one-third of the Choctaw population would be moved each year over the three year period beginning November 1, 1831.

The Choctaw were required to leave all of their personal possessions, including livestock, with the promise that they would be paid for everything upon their arrival in their new homeland. This proved to be a false promise for many. They were to report to two designated ferry points along the Mississippi River. In the meantime, the Bureau of Indian Affairs offered special incentives to those who would walk the hundreds of miles to their new home. These incentives included ten dollars in gold, a new rifle, three months' supply of ammunition and gunpowder, food along the trail and a qualified guide. Approximately 300 Choctaw accepted the offer to walk. Many of them would perish along the way, led off the route by their incompetent guide and caught in a blizzard while lost in a 30 mile-long swamp.

Those who chose to be transported fared little better. Lack of proper planning and execution by government officials, made worse by freezing temperatures, heavy rains and blizzards, took their toll on the Choctaw migrants. There were numerous missteps concerning ferries to be used to transport the Choctaw across the Mississippi. Food shortages and lack of clothing and blankets, coupled with white man diseases, such as cholera and dysentery, resulted in deaths of countless men, women and children. Many of the children were exposed to the harsh elements completely naked. At one point, both the Choctaw and their soldier escorts were limited to a daily ration of one handful of boiled or parched corn, one turnip and two cups of heated water.

In a newspaper interview, one of the Choctaw chiefs stated that the removal to that point had been "a trail of tears and death." Thus, the entire travail became known as the "Trail of Tears," because of the hardship, suffering and death experienced by the participants. The term became embedded in the American consciousness with the subsequent removal of the Cherokee in 1838.

Government planners learned little from the bitter experiences of the first year, continuing the schedule for subsequent phases of the removal during the late fall and winter months, with much the same results. However, there were no floods during the 1833 phase, making it somewhat more bearable than the 1831 and 1832 removal efforts.

By 1871, most tribes in the U.S. had signed treaties ceding most or all of their ancestral land in exchange for reservations and welfare. But, under the General Allotment Act of 1887, the government changed its Indian policy once more, making tribal members individual landowners and farmers, thus, encouraging their absorption into white society. Some 138 million acres of reservation land were subdivided into tracts of 40-160 acres and allotted on an individual basis. The surplus was sold to white settlers. However, title to land allotted to Native Americans can be inherited by the owners' descendants. For example, Rev. Bobb and his family retain mineral rights to property allotted to his late father.

The name Oklahoma literally means "home of the red

people," reflecting its strong Indian culture and its large Indian population. Some 65-70 different Indian tribes have been represented historically in the state. Tuskahoma, originally spelled "Tushka Homma," the historic site of the Choctaw Nation Headquarters, literally means "red warrior." While Tuskahoma continues to function as the site for Council meetings and certain ceremonial activities, the administrative headquarters for the Choctaw Nation, also known as the Choctaw Tribal Complex, is located at Durant, Oklahoma.

Prior to 1979, leadership of the Choctaw Nation was appointed by the Secretary of the Bureau of Indian Affairs. Since ratification of the Choctaw Constitution that year, the chief has been elected by popular vote of members of the nation. A council member from each of the twelve districts within the nation is elected by voters within the district. They serve four-year terms. In addition to the chief, who represents the executive branch, and the Council, which is the legislative branch, there is a judicial branch. It consists of the chief justice, who must be a licensed attorney, and two associate justices who may be laymen. All are appointed by the chief. Their authority extends only to civil matters. Criminal cases are handled by civil authorities.

The Choctaw Nation sponsors some three dozen service programs, including adult education, higher education, child welfare, vocational development and relocation assistance, economic development, social and health services and special programs relating to agriculture, forestry, ranch operations and self-governance. It also sponsors more than 30 economic development ventures, many of them related to tourism, recreation and child care and development.

Rev. Bobb served as a council member from 1979-1997, when he was appointed chaplain of the Choctaw Nation. His position and role in Tribal Council matters attest to the high regard the Council and his people have for him and his service to them.

Chapter Eight

Over the centuries, the Choctaw, as well as other Native American tribes have suffered incalculable hardships, cruelties and injustices. They have been deceived and abused and some have been tortured or murdered. But, in spite of the past, many Choctaw have demonstrated a resilient spirit, which is in keeping with the Christian teaching of forgiveness and reconciliation.

Despite his age and failing sight, Rev. Bobb is an optimist who prefers to look toward the future rather than dwell on the past. He feels that Biblical prophecy is being fulfilled and that we are approaching the end times described throughout the Holy Bible, particularly in the book of Revelation. Thus, he feels it is important to reap God's harvest while there is still time. "The field is there and it is ripe for harvest," Rev. Bobb explained. "But it takes time, lots of time," he added. Ministering to his native people is a long-term commitment because it is essential to establish personal relationships and credibility in order to be effective. This is why Rev. Bobb is committed to following the leadership of the Holy Spirit as long as necessary and for as long as his strength and health permit.

While he is spiritually burdened for the vast majority of his people who do not know Jesus Christ as their personal Savior, his primary goal is to reach as many Choctaw youth as possible. This explains the emphasis upon camping, outdoor activities and other youth activities in CIM and the Bertram Bobb Bible Camp.

"I am committed to stay with it as long as possible," Rev. Bobb declared. And with his optimism, his strong voice and his zeal for winning his people to Christ, he could continue for a long time to come.

CRUICIFIED WITH CHRIST

I have been crucified with Christ and
it is no longer I who live, but Christ lives
in me; and the life I now live in the flesh
I live by faith in the Son of God who loved
me and delivered Himself up for me.

Galatians 2:20

A HIDING PLACE

My soul has a special place
Which knows no metes or bounds
There it escapes both time and space
Far from life's maddening sounds

The sun is more golden
The sky is more blue
To no one I'm beholden
When this place I view

Every soul needs such a retreat
A place to forego life's stress
A time with destiny to meet
When striving is laid to rest

This is where my soul can aspire
To whatever God has in store
Soaring above our mortal mire
Toward His eternal gift and more

Vina Harvey Coleman

Vina Harvey Coleman's Spiritual Journey

Chapter One

Vina Harvey Coleman's paternal grandfather arrived in America as a nursing infant in his mother's arms. They were passengers aboard a ship transporting slaves from the western coast of Africa to Virginia. The family does not have a record of their exact origin, but it is believed to have been from the area, which today is known as Guinea, Sierra Leone, Liberia or other states along the "Gold Coast." This is where most of the slave trade originated in the late Eighteenth and early Nineteenth Centuries.

According to a Public Broadcasting System documentary series, "Africans In America," originated through WGBH, Boston, some 10-12 million Africans were sold into slavery between the Fifteenth and Nineteenth Centuries. Historians have calculated that as many as half of them may have been brought to the New World, most of them sold to plantations owners and colonies in the Caribbean and South America as labor for production of sugar cane and other crops. About 240,000 are believed to have been brought directly to the United States. Mrs. Coleman's grandfather and great grandmother were among them

Slavery had existed for thousands of years in various parts of the world. Some of the earliest slaves were debtors and prisoners of war. And while the enslaved initially included people of many different ethnic backgrounds, the slave trade would ultimately focus on Africa, which is where Mrs. Coleman's forebears originated.

The story of slavery is a dark chapter in some six thousand years of man's recorded history. According to World Book Encyclopedia, it involved many different empires and nations, including the Greeks and Romans, as well as Spain, Portugal, Holland, France, Great Britain and of course, the United States. It was driven by politics as well as economics, social struggles and diverse other interests. For example, the Greeks sometimes purchased slaves from pirate ships. In the Roman Empire, slavery flourished as the Roman legions expanded their conquests. And there were instances when the poor would sell their own children for money to satisfy debts.

According to World Book, Spain was a dominant factor in slaving during the Sixteenth Century as it sought to provide labor for its colonies in places such as Brazil, and Portuguese ships were only too happy to oblige. The Dutch became a major factor in the slave trade during the Sixteenth Century, followed by the British, who by the late Eighteenth Century accounted for approximately half of the slaves brought to the New World. During this period, British ships were transporting up to 45,000 slaves per year to the New World.

"Africans In America" reported that some 54,000 voyages were made by Europeans for the purpose of buying and selling slaves. A typical voyage lasted from 60-120 days during which the enslaved were subjected to the most inhumane treatment and conditions. They were crammed between decks, shackled together, without adequate food, enduring unsanitary conditions, disease and even whippings by the crew. Many slaves went mad and chose to jump overboard rather than endure such indignities and mistreatment.

By the year 1860 there were almost four million slaves in the United States and they were located primarily, though not exclusively, in the fifteen Southern states because of the region's agrarian economic base. While the U. S. Congress enacted a law in 1807, which banned importation of slaves into the country beginning the next year, slavery was not officially abolished until President Abraham Lincoln's Emancipation Proclamation of 1863 freed the Southern slaves. But, slaves in other parts of the nation were not freed until adoption of the Thirteenth Amendment to the U.S. Constitution.

Following the end of the Civil War in 1865, the Fourteenth and Fifteenth Amendments to the Constitution were ratified, giving former slaves citizenship and civil rights.

However, the fact that Mrs. Coleman's great grandmother and her grandfather are believed by the family to have arrived in the United States after implementation of the law banning importation of slaves, may indicate that the law was not always strictly enforced. In any event, as an infant, her grandfather-to-be had no recollection of the hardship and stress endured by his mother and the other indentured passengers aboard the ship. He did learn, however, the ship was owned by two brothers, whose surname was Harvey. That is why he was given the surname "Harvey," thus, becoming Nathan Harvey. And he began life in America in the humblest and most inauspicious circumstances imaginable.

While the family has no written record of his arrival, they are certain it was sometime around the middle of the Nineteenth Century since Mr. Harvey died in 1938 at the approximate age of 100. Neither is there a clear record of the terms of his mother's bondage or how she and her son would eventually find their way to Bellville, Texas, a small farming and ranching community in the south central portion of the state.

It is likely that their migration to Texas occurred after the end of the Civil War in 1865 and during the reconstruction period following the war. There is little genealogical information, except family lore passed from one generation to the next, to document the family's transition from their status as slaves to that of freeholders. Freeholder is a term denoting those who own property for themselves. It is in contrast to being property owned by others. But, however it occurred, the transition was the beginning of a family spiritual legacy, which would continue with the birth of Nathan Harvey, Jr., Mrs. Coleman's father, and subsequent generations.

Despite their family's humble beginning as slaves and later, as sharecroppers, workers who tilled land belonging to others in return for a share of the crops, Mrs. Coleman, a sister and six brothers would be reared in a spiritually oriented family which would provide educational opportunities for their children, where none had previously existed. All eight Harvey children would graduate from high school and Mrs. Coleman would earn two degrees from Prairie View A&M, a predominantly black college, now a part of the Texas A&M University System. And this spiritual upbringing, coupled with her educational achievements, would lead Mrs. Coleman into a lifelong work, teaching, inspiring young people and service as a humble, dedicated lay leader in her community and her church.

Chapter Two

Vina Harvey Coleman was born on a farm in Bellville, Texas during the Great Depression of the 1930s. Despite the fact that this was also a period in which Texas, and indeed, most of America, was racially segregated, her father, Nathan Harvey, Jr., managed to provide a good quality of life for his family. There was plenty of food on the family dining table. And there was a spirit of love and sharing among family members. Through hard work and perseverance, Mr. Harvey was able to acquire ownership of some 35 acres of farmland. Though money was scarce, he and his family raised cattle, pigs, chickens and turkeys. They also grew corn and assorted vegetables to supplement their food supply. Mr. Harvey also raised cotton, which he sold as a money crop to generate income for the family.

The Harvey family lived in a large frame house, built on piers and beams. Thus, it sat above the ground and the area beneath the house created an irresistible attraction to the children. Mrs. Coleman can recall playing hide and seek under the house and also using the area as a refuge to escape occasional punishment for disobeying her parents. The house, which is still owned by descendants of the Harvey family, was so solidly constructed that it has withstood numerous natural disasters, including a tornado. It was designed with large open spaces inside rather than with defined rooms. Thus, the interior was dotted with nooks and crannies where family members would store personal possessions and seek some degree of privacy. The homestead was adjoined by small plots of land and houses owned by Mr. Harvey's siblings and other family members, creating a sense of family and community.

Their extended family gathers for periodic reunions, usually around the Memorial Day holiday, when they can visit and pay homage to their late parents, Mr. and Mrs. Nathan Harvey, Jr., who are buried in a nearby community cemetery, on land once owned by the family. Other reunions, usually attended by 40-50 of the Harvey siblings and their families are also held in other locations.

Mrs. Coleman has vivid memories of her childhood, especially the delicious food which her mother, Elittie Williams Harvey, prepared for the family on a wood burning kitchen stove. "Mother was a great cook and we always had enough food," Mrs. Coleman recalled. Her mother's fried chicken was her favorite. But, she also remembers the hams, sausages and other delicacies which her father cured in their own "smoke house," and which her mother served regularly to the family. The family fare also included fruit such as pears, peaches and plums, either fresh or "canned" in glass jars to preserve them for the off-season, and fresh vegetables, such as corn and beans grown in the family garden. Many of Mrs. Harvey's canning and preserving skills were acquired through her participation in the Texas A&M Extension Service home demonstration program.

In order to generate income for the family, Mr. Harvey would grow cotton and other money crops on his 35 acres. Also, he would cultivate tracts belonging to other landowners in return for a portion of crops. As a child, Mrs. Coleman recalls helping to thin rows of corn with a hoe, pick cotton and perform other work, both on the family farm and for other landowners. "But, we never were permitted to skip school in order to work," she explained.

Mrs. Coleman remembers her mother as tall and slender, with long straight hair. She wore long dresses and was always neat, setting an example for her family. Her father was also somewhat slender and slightly shorter than her mother. They were both committed to their family and to the leadership of the Holy Spirit, as evidenced by the spiritual atmosphere of their home, as well as their commitment to providing educational opportunities for their children.

Chapter Three

❦

Even though the Harvey family had little money and enjoyed no real luxuries, the parents recognized that educational opportunity was the key to a better quality of life for their children. Thus, they insisted on regular school attendance by their eight children, even though neither of them had the opportunity to attend school beyond the first few elementary grades.

The only school for black students in the Bellville suburb of Burleigh, where the family lived, was an elementary school, which provided classes through the fifth grade. There was no middle or high school for black students in their immediate area. This prompted Mrs. Coleman's parents to send her to live for a while with a family friend in nearby LaGrange, where she could continue her education. Later, she was sent to live with an aunt in Houston where she attended Jack Yates High School in the Houston Independent School District. Following her aunt's death, she would go to live with a family friend in Hempstead, a small rural town north of Houston, where she earned her high school diploma. Her parents paid a small amount of rent for Mrs. Coleman and her sister to share a bedroom with the lady who owned the house. But, they bought and prepared their own food. All the while, their mother was working to get authorities to establish a high school for black students near their home in the Bellville area. She was successful just as Mrs. Coleman was graduating from Sam Schwartz High School in Hempstead.

Despite the hardship and loneliness of living away from home and having to assume adult responsibilities at an early age, Mrs. Coleman was a good student and was popular with classmates. She was elected school "queen" during her senior year. Her best subjects were science and math and since a sister-in-law was a nurse, she decided to enroll in Prairie View A&M to pursue a career in nursing. However, her interest gravitated more toward business, so she switched her major and earned a degree in business administration. But, at the time, there were few, if any, job opportunities for black women with business degrees. So, she decided to become a teacher and returned to Prairie View where she earned a degree in elementary education.

While attending Prairie View, Mrs. Coleman was forced to continue her frugal lifestyle. In contrast to contemporary style-conscious college students, she wore hand-me-down clothes given to her by family members and friends. Her parents would visit the campus periodically, bringing food and other necessities from home. They would arrive on campus in an old hearse which Mr. Harvey had purchased after it had been converted into a mini bus. Mr. Harvey was able to make extra money by using the bus to provide transportation to and from school for neighboring students. The arrival of Mr. and Mrs. Harvey on campus, in the old hearse filled with food, was always greeted with great fanfare by their daughter and her friends.

It was while a student at Prairie View that Mrs. Coleman would meet and marry Vernon Coleman, a World War II veteran of the U.S. Navy, who was returning to begin his college training following the war. She would interrupt her college career in order to marry Mr. Coleman and accompany him to his first teaching job in Greenville, Texas, east of Dallas. But after a short time and much soul searching, she and her husband eventually would return to the Bellville area and Mrs. Coleman would complete her college training.

After receiving her degree in education, Mrs. Coleman would accept a teaching position near Bellville. For three years, she taught in the Austin County Common Schools and later taught one year at the remodeled Grant School, which she attended as a child. The year was spent substituting for a teacher on medical leave. Her most vivid memory of that year concerned a "pot belly" stove used to heat the classroom. She was not familiar with starting fires since her father always had the fires made and the house warm before she awakened for school each morning. So, she would place wood on top of old papers before lighting them. Almost invariably, smoke would cloud the room and she and her students would be forced to go outside until the smoke had cleared. Often they would rush to the windows and door for fresh air. Then she would return and fan the fire until the flames started and warmed the room. Only then would class work begin. Her first fulltime job after moving to Austin and before returning to her teaching career was as director of a daycare center, Children's Haven. Subsequently, she taught for 13 years in the Austin Independent School District in Travis County. An injury sustained while supervising a physical education class would end her teaching career. But, it would open the door to new opportunities for teaching and for spiritual leadership.

Chapter Four

Mrs. Coleman was reared in a family atmosphere where spiritual matters and core values were observed and taught. Prayers of thanksgiving always preceded mealtimes. The family would stand around the breakfast table each morning and every member participated in reading of the scriptures and prayer. Each day would end with prayers before going to bed. Mr. and Mrs. Harvey set the example for their children by kneeling at their bed each night to pray. To this day, Mrs. Coleman continues the ritual of prayer in both the morning and evening. On Sundays, she and her husband spend time together in prayer. "I don't care how busy I am, I must pray and talk to God each day," she declared.

The Harvey family attended Bethlehem Baptist Church in the small community of Burleigh, near Bellville. This church, which still has an active congregation today, is where Mrs. Coleman would publicly profess her faith in Jesus Christ as her Lord and Savior. And it was here that she would acquire the spiritual foundation, which has supported her lifelong commitment as a disciple of Christ.

Somewhat precocious and a fast learner, Mrs. Coleman became spiritually aware at an early age. Even before she started school at age six, she had told her parents of her desire to make a public profession of faith in Christ and to join the church. However, there was a feeling among some of the church leadership that she was too young for such an important decision and that she should wait until she was older and more mature.

Several years later, at the age of ten, Vina Harvey sat in church one Sunday morning, listening to a sermon delivered by a visiting minister. She desperately wanted to respond when an altar call would be issued at the close of the service. In the midst of her uncertainty, the minister made direct eye contact with her, which she interpreted as a direct invitation from God. This gave her the assurance she needed to walk down the aisle when an invitation was extended by the minister. When the invitation was extended she came forward to make what would be the most important decision of her life. It was the decision to accept Jesus Christ as her Lord and Savior and to follow the leadership of the Holy Spirit throughout her life.

A short time later, the ten year-old and a group of other converts would be baptized, a ritual described in the New Testament, which involves submersion in water as a symbolic burial of the unredeemed life and resurrection to a new spiritual life in Christ. (Matthew 3:11). Since Bethlehem Baptist Church did not have a formal baptismal pool inside its sanctuary, the baptismal service was conducted on a nearby farm, in an earthen tank used to provide water for livestock. The service was held on a Sunday afternoon, following morning services at the church. Mrs. Coleman has vivid memories of the white gown she wore as she was submersed in the somewhat muddy water of the tank. But, more importantly, she recalls the support of family members and friends who shared this important spiritual milestone with her. She recalls the congregation singing a hymn, "On Jordan's Stormy Banks." She also remembers looking up from the water to see a herd of cattle staring at the proceedings with stoic, yet quizzical expressions.

It was customary in Bethlehem Baptist Church and among family and friends to share the good news of such important spiritual decisions in a very direct and personal manner. Thus, after traditional revival meetings, usually held during the summer months, and at various times throughout the year, new converts would visit the homes of friends, relatives and neighbors to share the good news of their decisions and declare their faith in Christ. In keeping with the Biblical admonition to profess faith in Christ publicly, this was considered an important part of each individual's spiritual journey and commitment. Mrs. Coleman gladly shared her decision and her faith and this experience would help her in witnessing to others in the years to come.

Chapter Five

Vernon Coleman grew up in Galveston, Texas. An only child, he was drafted into military service during World War II as a teenager. He spent three years in the U.S. Navy, most of it aboard a ship in the Pacific Theatre of operations. Following his discharge from military service, Mr. Coleman used benefits from the GI Bill of Rights to enroll first in Langston College in Oklahoma, later transferring to Prairie View A&M. There he majored in industrial arts and following his graduation, he accepted a teaching position in the Greenville, Texas school district. His new bride would accompany him, interrupting her own college studies to be with her new husband. But, she was not happy being out of school or living in Greenville, despite the fact that she occasionally worked as a substitute teacher in the same school system where her husband taught.

It was during this difficult transition time that the new bride would rely on her prayer life for consolation and guidance. She felt that she and her new husband were not in the place where God wanted them to be. "So, I did a lot of praying," she explained. She recalls that "One morning I awoke and as always began the day with a prayer. I knelt beside my bed in my usual manner. As I began to pray I felt what seemed to be a hard strike under the bottoms of my feet, followed by what appeared to be a veil thrown over my head. I leaped to my feet, very frightened. Sensing that the Holy Spirit was speaking to me, I stood scared and amazed. Fear immediately left, tears began to flow and I was inspired to cover my mouth so I could not be heard." Following His direction, she began to understand that those who truly have faith in Christ and the indwelling of the Holy Spirit are assured of divine guidance in all of their relationships and activities. It was at this point that the new bride would make a renewed commitment to remain open to His guidance in her life, however and wherever He might lead. This is the first time she has shared this story. It was another milestone in her spiritual journey. And to this day, Mrs. Coleman makes certain that her feet are covered when she prays and that the lights are burning as a symbol of His enlightened leadership for her life.

After several years in Greenville, Mr. Coleman would transfer to the LaMarque School district, near his Galveston home, and his wife would return to Prairie View A&M to complete her teaching degree. Following her graduation, she would serve as a substitute teacher in LaMarque, before accepting a fulltime teaching position in Bellville. They would later teach in the Austin Independent School District in the Texas capital city. It was here that he would retire after 32 years in the classroom and she would leave the classroom following an injury sustained while teaching a physical education class.

While Mrs. Coleman was still teaching in Austin, she and Mr. Coleman would drive to Bellville to visit family after morning services each Sunday. During these 90 minute drives, with her husband at the wheel, Mrs. Coleman would plan her teaching agenda for the coming week and study for her responsibilities as a youth leader at her church, Ebenezer Baptist Church near downtown Austin. It was at these times that Mrs. Coleman felt the Holy Spirit's direction, telling her she was too busy and that she was not devoting enough time and energy to the things He wanted her to do.

A short time later, while supervising a dodge ball game in the school gymnasium, Mrs. Coleman was hit in the face by a stray ball. Knocked unconscious, she sustained a neck injury, which ultimately forced her to quit teaching fulltime. Was it Divine intervention? Mrs. Coleman is not sure. But, she is certain that when God wants one of his followers in a particular ministry or place, He will put them there, even when His will appears to be inconsistent with the individual's personal priorities.

Chapter Six

❧

After leaving her public school teaching position, Mrs. Coleman eventually was led to the Austin Baptist Association, an organization of more than 135 Baptist churches in Central Texas. At first, she worked as a staff member, assisting the Association in its mission to help member churches in developing and strengthening their outreach programs. She would resign as a fulltime staff member to devote more time to her family and church. However, she would remain involved as a volunteer, later being named director of discipleship training. And it was through this position that her influence would be felt by individuals and churches throughout Central Texas.

As a member of the Association staff, she had a spiritual impact not only on those served by the Association, but also on her co-workers. David W. Smith, executive director of ABA, said he is most impressed by her level of commitment. "For more than 25 years, Vina Coleman has volunteered to do whatever needs to be done," he explained. "She has a tremendous heart for service and a level of commitment which is very unusual," he added. The Rev. Frank Deutsch, formerly director of church services and Christian social ministries at ABA, said the most important aspect of Mrs. Coleman's spiritual leadership is that it is "real." "Vina believes in walking the Christian walk, not just talking it,"

Deutsch declared. He said he had been inspired by both her personal life and her service to others. Deutsch has since retired from ABA and is now pastor of Austin Baptist Chapel, which provides a soup kitchen ministry, including two Sunday services, for Austin's inner-city needy.

When Mrs. Coleman joined Ebenezer Baptist Church more than 40 years ago, it was the continuation of a spiritual journey which would enable her to influence the lives of at least two generations of youth, while also helping strengthen the congregations of numerous local churches. Centrally located near downtown Austin, Ebenezer Baptist draws worshippers from the entire metropolitan area. Thus, her influence would be spread through this century old institution.

Mrs. Coleman's concern for the spiritual lives of young people was driven in part by the mentoring of her daughter, Vernie, who is now Mrs. Dennis Coleman Daniels of Atlanta, Georgia. Mrs. Daniels was graduated from the University of Texas, where she met her future husband, Dr. Dennis Daniels. Later, she would earn a degree in pharmacy from Texas Southern University in Houston, and her master's degree from Butler University in Indianapolis, Indiana. Her husband would receive his medical degree from the University of Texas School of Public Health in Houston. Dr. Daniels, who is also an ordained minister, is an epidemiologist, currently serving as deputy director of the Fulton County Health and Wellness Department in Atlanta, Ga. They are parents of three sons. Being the grandmother of three has also strengthened Mrs. Coleman's concern for youth.

Mrs. Coleman's spiritual leadership began as a Sunday School teacher while she was a student at Prairie View A&M. When she and her husband joined Ebenezer Baptist in 1960, there was a need for Sunday School teachers, as well as leaders for a Sunday evening program, then named Baptist Training Union. She began teaching classes in both

Sunday School and BTU. And using her background as a professional educator, she knew how to engage students, involving them in activities of interest as a prelude to Bible study. Her home was a favorite gathering place for young people, especially her daughter and friends. And there was always plenty of home cooked food as well as a sympathetic ear for those who had problems they wished to confide in someone other than their own parents.

Support from her family has always been an important part of Mrs. Coleman's spiritual life. Daughter Vernie learned to play the piano, a skill, which now enables her to complement her husband's ministerial activities. And her willing participation in church activities was a magnet for other youth, as well. Husband Vernon has also been supportive, sometimes serving as chauffeur, sounding board for ideas and artist for various programs. He plays bass guitar and sings in the Ebenezer choir and male chorus.

Mrs. Coleman's spiritual influence has reached far beyond her own community. As youth director at her church, she has led Bible drill and youth speaker's tournament programs. For several years, some members of her groups won statewide competition and several participants were invited to speak at the Baptist Conference Center in Glorieta, New Mexico. But, her greatest satisfaction has been the opportunity to influence the lives of several generations of young people. For example, she was inspired by a recent visit from a young man whom she had taught while he was a student at the University of Texas. He brought his family to visit the Coleman home, where he had enjoyed so many home cooked meals and activities with others his own age.

Chapter Seven

Mrs. Coleman carries out her responsibilities as discipleship training director for the Austin Baptist Association on a regular basis. Her days may be spent telephoning church leaders, inquiring about their mission programs and any needs they may have for assistance. Or she may speak at a church meeting or conference of churches, encouraging the establishment of outreach programs and instructing local lay leaders. And in order to assure that she is following the leadership of the Holy Spirit, each day includes time for Bible study and prayer. The mission of the Association is "Assisting member churches in their individual efforts to advance the Kingdom of God." And her role is central to carrying out this mission. But, her primary concern continues to be for young people living in an increasingly complex contemporary society.

One of the greatest needs of young people today, Mrs. Coleman believes, is for someone who will listen to them. "We need to spend more time listening to young people and talking about what is troubling to them," she declared. They need non-judgmental understanding and encouragement, she added.

Based on her experience, Mrs. Coleman believes that religious music, contemporary versus traditional, is an important concern for today's youth. Thus, church leaders should be more flexible in music selection in order to attract their interest, she said. Also, young people need and want more instruction about other religions and how they compare to Christianity.

As Mrs. Coleman enters her seventh decade, her energy and enthusiasm for helping meet the spiritual needs of others through the leadership of the Holy Spirit remain strong and vibrant. And she has committed her service as a disciple of Christ in keeping with the leadership of the Holy Spirit.

HE CHOSE YOU

You did not choose me, but I chose you
and appointed you that you should go
and bear fruit, and that your fruit should
remain, that whatever you ask of the
Father in My name, He may give to you.

John 15:16

REPENTANCE

I wandered far
From 'neath the cross
My soul was marred
By life's dull dross

When weary of things
Without true meaning
God gave me wings
To soar above mortal leaning

Now free of guilt
My joy is complete
Whatever His will
I will strive to meet

William O. Bolen

William O. Bolen's Spiritual Journey

Chapter One

William O. "Bill" Bolen cannot identify any single event or relationship, which has shaped the course of his spiritual journey. As with most individuals, many relationships and circumstances have influenced his life over three quarters of a century. But, just as a pebble tossed into a pond creates a wide ripple over the surface of the water, and a gentle breeze can stir the branches of a mighty tree, some of life's seemingly insignificant relationships and events can prove to be providential in their impact.

It was just such a casual relationship as a small boy, which had a profound impact upon the course of his life. Afternoons after school and during long, hot summer days in the Alabama black belt, so named for the color of the soil, Bolen would spend many hours playing with friends, one of whom was Neva Kaiser, a neighbor. Neva's parents, Mr. and Mrs. E.L. Kaiser, lived in a modest house located behind a grocery store and service station operated by Bolen's parents.

Frequently, when Bolen would stop by the Kaiser home to

visit Neva and her older sister, Juanita, the girls would be away visiting other friends. He would wander into the house and find Mrs. Kaiser, affectionately known as "Mada," who could usually be found in the kitchen. There she might be baking, washing dishes or preparing her family's evening meal. Mada was relatively short, slightly overweight and her brown hair was streaked with gray, all of which reinforced her motherly demeanor. One of her specialties, which was usually in good supply, was tea cakes, a cookie sized, crispy pastry with just enough sugar to please the palate of a small boy. And she would always offer Bolen his choice of whatever was available.

"This wonderful Christian lady had a very fine way about her and an unusual ability to communicate with young people. So, I was always very comfortable being around her and talking with her," Bolen recalled. "We talked about many things, but I specifically remember our conversations about the importance of doing things which are right, rather than doing things which are wrong. Mada would impress upon me the reasons for doing right and she would always use Jesus Christ as an example, describing how He stood for right. I can also remember her teaching me to say blessings at the table before meals and how to pray," he said. "These conversations in the kitchen over a period of years were a strong influence in my life and they helped lead me to accept Jesus Christ as my personal savior," he explained.

It was a chance relationship, which seemingly was of little consequence. But, the concern and witness of this sincere Christian lady and her family would have a lasting impact upon Bolen's life and his spiritual witness for many years to come.

Chapter Two

B ill Bolen was born on the wrong side of the tracks in the small south central Alabama town of Selma. It was during the late nineteen twenties, just prior to the onset of the Great Depression in 1929. During this period, desirable housing was difficult to find almost everywhere. Selma was no exception. There was an east-west division in Selma at the time. Those who lived west of Broad Street, the main thoroughfare, were on the "right" side of the railroad tracks, which ran through the town. Residents on the east side of Broad were considered to be "across the tracks." But, after living in the Hotel Albert for three months after moving from Tuscaloosa to Selma, Bolen's parents, the late Mr. and Mrs. J. Ben Bolen, were not concerned about status when a house across the tracks was completed and ready for sale. Besides, Bolen's father worked for the railroad and the tracks were a symbol of economic security. So, the Bolen family moved into the house at 2000 Franklin Street and it was here that Bill Bolen was born. He had two older brothers, Ben, Jr., and Frank. A sister had died in infancy.

Despite what some who were concerned with status might perceive as a modest, or even deprived beginning, Bolen was born into a stable, loving middle class family. At times the family may have been short on cash, but when times got tough, they stuck together and demonstrated character and resourcefulness which are shared by many American families in similar circumstances. After Bolen's father was laid off from his job at the railroad, he operated a small grocery store and service station to support the family. His mother worked alongside his father to make the business successful. They operated the store for about 12 years, until his father was rehired by the railroad. Thus, living "across the tracks" and having to adjust to the ups and downs of an economy plagued by an unprecedented depression meant that Bolen and his family were like most other American families. And since they do not trace their genealogy to any specific ethnic or cultural lineage, they can identify with the melting pot, which is represented by the largest segment of American society.

Selma provided a friendly, small town quality of life where people of different origins and backgrounds lived harmoniously. Its image would be tarnished by the highly publicized march across the Edmund Pettus Bridge, spanning the Alabama River, during the civil rights demonstrations which dotted the American landscape more than a quarter of a century later. But, the caricature of Selma as the site of racial strife was not an accurate reflection of the town or its residents, either then or now.

The Bolen home had a wide porch shaded by a large elm tree and several pecan trees. On one side were a stand of oak trees and a dahlia garden. In the backyard there was a variety of fruit trees. It was typical of most of the other homes in Selma, even if it was "across the tracks." And it provided a warm family atmosphere, which would nurture Bolen and his brothers through their formative years.

It was this family nurturing, in a small town setting, which would help shape Bolen's character and start his spiritual pilgrimage as a student at the University of Alabama, later as a commissioned officer in the U.S. Air Force Reserve and finally his emergence as a Christian layman and radio and television personality in Birmingham, Alabama.

Chapter Three

❦

B olen would make the most important spiritual decision
of his life on Easter Sunday, 1940, at the age of 12. He
had been thinking about his spiritual life and his relationship
to Jesus Christ over a period of time. And he had discussed
his desire to make a profession of faith in Christ with both
his parents and his pastor.

Easter Sunday dawned bright, sunny and hot, assuring
the traditionally large attendance at the morning service at
Selma's First Baptist Church. Bolen sat through the service,
anxiously awaiting the closing hymn, when an invitation
would be extended to those wishing to make professions of
faith or other spiritual decisions. Traditionally, Easter Sunday
was a time when many people, especially youngsters like
Bolen, made public professions of faith. And this Easter was
no exception. Responding immediately to the pastor's invitation, Bolen made his way down the aisle, along with a number of others, some his own age. "It was meaningful, but it
was not a dramatic thing at all," Bolen recalled. It was, however, a commitment, which would subsequently shape the
course of his life.

Growing up in a spiritual atmosphere, under the influence of Christian parents, it is entirely possible that Bolen
would have accepted Christ and followed the leadership of
the Holy Spirit even without the interest and witness of

Mada Kaiser. It is true, nevertheless, that the concern of this Godly woman, coming as it did from outside his own family circle, would have a dramatic impact upon him and influence his decision to led a spiritually directed life.

Mrs. Kaiser was not particularly well educated. Her husband, known to Bolen and other friends as "Ern," was a tall, thin, unassuming man who earned a modest income as a craftsman, working in a machine shop. Ern smoked a pipe, told funny stories and enjoyed teasing Bolen, frequently lifting him up seated in the palms of his hands, grown coarse and strong from his daily work. The impact of their love and their Christian influence, however, was immeasurable. It demonstrated how the Holy Spirit can work through humble, responsive servants, regardless of their background or status.

Chapter Four

J ust as a seed requires nourishment and cultivation to produce a mature crop, so, too, must the human spirit be nurtured if it is to flourish. And as with many followers of Christ, spiritual growth for Bolen was a gradual, sometimes erratic process. Regular attendance at church services and other religious activities, the fellowship of Christian friends and participation in a prayer and Bible study group were all factors which helped Bolen develop his spiritual awareness and understand the tremendous resource which is available to Christians through the indwelling of the Holy Spirit.

Another strong influence on Bolen came from Clyde Beasley, a classmate. They met in junior high school and were immediately drawn to each other, perhaps to some extent by their physical differences. While they were about the same height, Beasley was husky, weighing about 15-20 pounds more than Bolen, who acquired the nickname "Frail," because of his thin build and frail appearance. Beasley was also jovial and outgoing in contrast to Bolen, who was somewhat less gregarious. Their friendship grew, not only through activities at school and church, but also when they were hired for after school jobs at the same grocery store. Earlier, Bolen had worked at his parents' store, but this was an assertion of his growing independence.

Continuing their friendship into their senior year in high

school, both youngsters felt a strong urge to enter fulltime Christian service as their vocation. Beasley subsequently became a Baptist minister. His close friend's decision to enter the ministry caused Bolen to seriously question whether he also was being spiritually led to become a minister. But, still uncertain about the ministry or a vocation in a church related field, he enrolled in the University of Alabama. There he majored in radio arts, now a part of the communications curriculum. It was possible, he thought, that the Holy Spirit might be leading him into a spiritual vocation through the medium of radio. There, he received his degree and was commissioned a second lieutenant in the U.S. Air Force Reserve. After serving a two-year tour on active duty, he continued as a member of the Air Force Reserve and Alabama Air National Guard until his retirement.

Still seeking the Holy Spirit's direction in his life, Bolen contacted the Baptist Radio and Television Commission, a part of the Southern Baptist Convention, to explore job opportunities following his release from active duty with the Air Force. However, the Commission was financially unable to employ fulltime staff members at the time, and this door of opportunity was closed. By this time, Bolen had married his college sweetheart, the former Vivian Kellebrew of Anniston, Alabama, and they had become parents of the first two of their four children. This made fulltime employment a necessity for the family breadwinner.

Thus, Bolen joined WSGN Radio in Birmingham, where he spent the next eleven years as a staff announcer and newsman. At the same time, he and Vivian and their children became active members of Birmingham's First Baptist Church. It was there where Bolen would be ordained as a Deacon and serve as director of Church Training, a Sunday evening equivalent of Sunday School, which is usually conducted on Sunday morning.

He would leave WSGN Radio to become news director

for a new television station in Birmingham, WBMG-TV. Later, First Baptist Church made a decision to sponsor a half-hour program on the station. It would include a five minute segment of religious news and Bolen was invited to handle this portion of the show. It was a sign of a door being opened for Bolen to combine his spiritual leanings with his vocational skills. He continued this program for about two years until he moved to another, larger television station, WBRC-TV, where he continues today, serving at times as a co-anchor on a morning newscast and performing other on-camera assignments as needed, while in semi-retirement.

About a year after joining WBRC-TV, Bolen was assigned to host a half hour weekly religious news program. Later, he would be asked to host a monthly religious discussion program. It provided in-depth interviews, panel discussions, and other techniques to make religious news relevant to a general television audience. While the programs have suffered the vagaries of television programming demands, they were opportunities which Bolen was uniquely suited to accept. And, undoubtedly, they were milestones in his life-long spiritual pilgrimage.

"About 20 years after I first felt this call, I realized that perhaps I was doing what the Holy Spirit was directing me to do," Bolen declared. Still seeking further evidence of spiritual guidance in his life, Bolen strongly considered accepting an offer of a position in the children's book division of the Southern Baptist Convention's publishing unit in Nashville, Tennessee. But, without strong spiritual direction to make a change, he and Vivian made the decision to continue making whatever spiritual contributions they could make through his television work and their activities through their church, Brookwood Baptist, in Mountain Brook, a Birmingham suburb. In addition to his church responsibilities, Bolen speaks at various religious and civic organization meetings. And both he and Vivian regularly

give their testimonies concerning life threatening illnesses
which they have survived with spiritual help.

Chapter Five

Vivian Bolen experienced a particularly difficult crisis in 1969 when she underwent radical cancer surgery. On Easter Sunday of that year, exactly 31 years after Bolen's profession of faith, Vivian discovered a fibroid breast tumor. She immediately consulted her physician and was scheduled for surgery to remove the tumor. About an hour after the surgery began, Bolen was summoned by their family doctor who was also his Sunday School teacher. "Bill, it was not as good as we had hoped. We need to continue with radical surgery with your permission." Several days would pass following the surgery before tests could confirm that it was completely successful. "Those days were an eternity which I could not have survived without faith in the power of the Holy Spirit," Bolen explained. Vivian's faith in her recovery was just as strong. Five years later, when tests indicated she had experienced no recurrence of the disease, both felt another spiritual door had opened for them.

However, Vivian would suffer a minor stroke and temporary loss of her speech and use of her hands about 19 months after the cancer surgery. She made a full recovery from the effects of the stroke, but in 1991, a routine physical examination would discover another breast tumor. Another surgery subsequently removed the tumor before it could spread to other portions of her body.

In the meantime, Bolen would face a physical and spiritual crisis of his own. In 1987, prior to embarking with Vivian on a long awaited vacation in Europe, Bolen consulted his physician for what he thought was a hereditary malady, a "nervous stomach." He was given medication and encouraged to take the vacation, but to have a consultation upon his return. Following his return, the physician conducted a colon exam during which he removed a series of polyps, most of which were benign. However, one proved to be malignant, which required major surgery involving a resection of the colon. While the malignancy had not spread and there was no need for chemotherapy or other continuing treatment, full recovery required several years.

These physical crises have been difficult for the Bolens. But the crises have also served to strengthen their faith. And they have provided opportunities for both Vivian and Bill to use their experiences to provide encouragement and hope for others facing similar problems. They do this by speaking to various groups individually and as a couple.

Chapter Six

A major influence in Bolen's decision to pursue a career in communications came from his participation in Sunday School. This could be interpreted as a way the Holy Spirit guides those who are faithful and receptive.

His Sunday School teacher, who was employed by a national retailer, suggested to Bolen that he might find a job in the shipping room of the local store. He did and this led to an event, which changed his life forever. The shipping room was adjacent to the radio repair shop where technicians also worked on a relatively new invention, the wire recorder, forerunner to the tape recorder. After checking out each new recorder, technicians would test it by recording messages. This provided an opportunity for Bolen and other employees to record their voices. One day after hearing Bolen's voice, the shipping room clerk asked if he had ever considered working in radio. He hadn't, but since he liked to perform in class plays and entertain classmates in other ways, Bolen began thinking about it. Since a classmate worked at the local radio station, Bolen asked him about job openings and this led to his first job in radio, as a part time announcer.

Bolen's years as a student at the University of Alabama provided opportunities for spiritual growth, as well as development of his professional communications skills. As a member of the University's Baptist Student Union and Calvary

Baptist Church, which also served the University community, Bolen interacted with other students who were seeking to lead spiritually directed lives. Frequently, he would participate in student groups, which would visit small churches in the area, leading worship services and providing other support. On one occasion, Bolen and several friends went to a small town south of the University where they had been invited to conduct a series of revival meetings over a weekend. Despite much prayer and preparation, the group conducted services on Friday evening, Saturday evening and Sunday morning without any professions of faith or decisions for church membership. Finally, there was a large response at the Sunday evening service, after which church leaders requested that the students continue the services into the next week. Monday evening's service brought similar results, after which the group agreed to commute from school in order to conduct additional services on Tuesday and Wednesday evenings. At the conclusion of the Wednesday service, 35 had made professions of faith and six had joined the church, transferring membership from churches elsewhere. The lesson was clear to the student leaders, as well as the local church leaders who had been constantly praying for the services. Faith, prayer and persistence can prevail in most situations.

Chapter Seven

Being aware of the indwelling of the Holy Spirit and remaining open and receptive to His direction is a challenge for every follower of Jesus Christ. Bolen and his family have been successful in remaining attuned to the Spirit's leadership in a number of ways. These include a spiritual atmosphere in the home, regular participation in church services and other religious activities, consistent prayer and Bible study, Christian role models and reaching out to others.

The Bolen family, which includes son, Bill, Jr., and daughters, Lory, Jenny, and Sandy, always observed a period of prayer and thanksgiving before meals. And there were open lines of communication for discussion of religious matters, school work, social activities or other concerns. Of course, regular church attendance was expected of everyone. A relaxed, supportive relationship between parents and children invited open discussion, sharing of concerns and a positive approach to problem solving. This served the family well in later years when a daughter and her husband discovered that some unethical dealings by a business partner threatened their family's financial security. The family closed ranks to address the problem and now they are helping rebuild the business.

Bolen's early morning work routine over the years made

scheduling time for family activities a difficult challenge. For most of those years, his workday would begin with a first alarm around 3:15 a.m. A second alarm was set for 3:30 a.m. just in case he failed to respond to the first. Quickly showering and dressing, he would make his way to the kitchen of his suburban Mountain Brook home for a breakfast of cereal, toast and coffee. Eating alone in the freshness of the morning, Bolen found time for meditation and prayer. And most mornings there was time for Bible study and reading of devotional materials. Resetting the alarm for 6:30 a.m. so that Vivian can get her day started on schedule, Bolen would make the 20-minute drive to the television studios, arriving around 4:45 a.m. This enabled him to prepare for his first newscast and assignments for the early morning show, "Good Day, Alabama." By mid-morning, Bolen would complete most of the day's on-camera work. The remainder of the day provided time for research, writing, and other duties in preparation for the next day. Later in the afternoon, there might be time for church activities or visits to a health club. After dinner at home with Vivian, Bolen was usually in bed by 9 p.m. so that he can make another early start the next day. Weekends and holidays still include time for visits with Bill, Jr., Lory, Jenny and Sandy and their families, which now include 10 grandchildren.

Reaching out to others includes participation in mission activities at his church. Bolen recalled a trip, which he and 25 other members of Brookwood Baptist Church made to Connecticut to assist a sister church in construction of a sanctuary. The group arrived to find the project behind schedule and not ready for their phase of the work. It was also discovered that appropriate permits had not been secured from local authorities. If the work could not proceed as scheduled, the Brookwood mission group would have made a long, expensive trip in vain.

Following extensive prayer sessions seeking divine

guidance, the group developed a strategy and went to work expediting completion of early phases of construction, contacting officials to get necessary permits, paying delinquent fees and completing the work they had come to do. Bolen described the accomplishment of their mission as something of a miracle and certainly, "an answer to prayer."

A number of other role models, such as "Mada" Kaiser, have also played an important part in helping Bolen develop a spiritually directed life. One was Malcolm Street, a Christian layman and radio executive in Vivian Bolen's hometown, Anniston, Alabama. While a student at the University of Alabama and for years afterward, Bill and Vivian would visit her parents at their Anniston home on weekends. They always attended church during these visits. Street, who was co-owner and general manager of WHMA Radio in Anniston, was teacher of the Sunday School class they would attend. Since Bolen was working part-time at the radio station in Selma and studying radio arts at the University, Street and Bolen were drawn to each other by their mutual interests. As their friendship developed, Bolen began to understand that in contrast to many others whom he had met in radio, it is possible to combine a strong spiritual life with a successful career in radio. "He was a marvelous man whose example has given me strength on many occasions when I sorely needed it," Bolen explained.

Still another strong influence on Bolen was the life of the late R.G. LeTourneau, a widely known Twentieth Century industrialist and dynamic Christian layman. LeTourneau authored a book entitled, "God Runs My Business," which spelled out his belief that no individual can outgive God. Thus, he kept ten percent of his income and gave 90 percent to his church and spiritual causes, in contrast to the Biblical teaching, which encourages giving a tithe or 10 percent to God. LeTourneau conducted a revival meeting at Bolen's church and his witness had a dramatic impact upon the youngster. Bolen's father was so impressed by LeTourneau that he bought a case of his books and gave them away to friends. After LeTourneau's death, his son Roy established a foundation to support the work of Christian missionaries. Bolen accompanied the younger LeTourneau on a weeklong trip to South America where the foundation was supporting a mission program in Lima, Peru. This helped him develop a heart for missions.

While Bolen made the decision to officially retire from his position at WBRC-TV in Birmingham late in 2001, he continues to work a reduced schedule at the station and is anything but retired. Well past normal retirement age, Bolen continues work not only because he enjoys it, but also because he feels this is what the Holy Spirit is leading him to do. "I hope I have done for other young people interested in radio and television, what Malcolm Street did for me," Bolen said. "And I hope I have conducted myself, both on and off the air, in a way which demonstrates that I consider the Holy Spirit as a role model, as well," he added.

Spiritual Reflections
Of The Author

One of my fondest childhood memories is of my mother singing in her kitchen as she made preparations for lunch for her family before attending Sunday morning church services. She would sometimes sing, other times hum, hymns or other religious songs as she busily prepared the meal, which would be ready to serve when the family returned home from church.

More often than not there would be a beef roast with savory brown gravy, green beans cooked with potatoes, creamed corn, stewed tomatoes, black eye peas or other fresh vegetables. And there would always be her signature yeast rolls, along with a dessert, such as her homemade, dark chocolate cake, referred to as "devil's food" in the vernacular. She developed a reputation for her rolls, which she shared with family and friends, regularly preparing them for meals prepared for friends during periods of bereavement or on other occasions. And she must have baked hundreds of "devil's food" cakes over the years, as well as pies and cakes of other assorted flavors.

At church, her clear soprano voice was a mainstay in the small choir. It was of such quality that had she been afforded the opportunity for voice training, she could have had a successful career in music. Because of her fluency in English and her writing skills, she served as church secretary for many years, recording business meeting minutes as a volunteer service, without pay.

Another Sunday morning ritual, when my father was not working in the steel mill where he was employed, was shining shoes in preparation for church. A stickler in his dress, my father always wore a neatly pressed shirt, tie and suit, and his shoes were always shined. This was a carryover from his childhood when he shined shoes on the street corner in the small Alabama town where he spent most of his youth. When asked how much money he had made shining shoes in any one day, he quickly replied, "five dollars and twenty cents." And what did he do with it? "I took it home to Mama," he said proudly. He was an ordained deacon in our small church and remained faithful in attendance and other service past his ninetieth year, as long as his health permitted. He died in 1999, just shy of his ninety-fourth birthday. My mother died two years earlier at the age of 89.

My parents were both from families with modest economic means. But they measured life in intrinsic values, rather than in terms of dollars. My mother's maiden name was Olean Moss. She was related through her mother, Jenny Hinchey Moss, to the Rev. John Pirtle, of Washington County, Kentucky. Rev. Pirtle had been born in Virginia of parents, Henry and Mary Pirtle, who were of German and Swedish extraction. Pirtle had settled on 100 acres of land, which he purchased in Washington County in 1796. One of the witnesses to the deed was Mordecai Lincoln, eldest brother of Thomas Lincoln, father of Abraham Lincoln. A family genealogical book, published in 1934, contains a report by Orval W. Baylor, a Lincoln historian of Springfield, Kentucky, concerning John Pirtle. Baylor reported that Pirtle often preached as a layman in the small

"Methodist Meeting House" on the banks of the Beech Fork River, where Thomas Lincoln and Nancy Hanks attended before they were married.

Baylor said "If any one man, more than another, left an indelible impression by his preaching upon the hearts and minds of Thomas Lincoln and Nancy Hanks, that man was John Pirtle." He also said if Pirtle had been an ordained minister in 1806, he probably would have been called upon to perform the marriage ceremony of Lincoln and Hanks. Pirtle was ordained on October 12, 1812 by the Methodist Episcopal Church in recognition of his services "as an exponent of Methodism and organizer of congregations of that faith."

My father, Howard Clayton Harris, was born of Irish-Scottish heritage on a farm in East Mississippi. His mother's surname was Gordon, whose family can be traced to Scotland. As a small boy, he moved to a small West Alabama town, Carbon Hill, with his family. After completing high school, he became a land surveyor for the Alabama Highway Department and moved to Birmingham where he met my mother. She had moved there from Kentucky with her family. After graduating from high school, she began working in a local bank.

Their struggles in rearing a family prior to and during the aftermath of the Great Depression of 1929 and their commitment to living disciplined lives, sacrificing for their family, while giving generously of their time and their limited means to the church, made an indelible impression upon my spiritual awareness. Growing up in this kind of family atmosphere contributed to my making a profession of faith in Jesus Christ, at the age of 10 during a community revival service. Even though I maintained church membership and regular attendance throughout my adolescent and young adult years, it was not until I was well into adulthood that I became more fully aware of the true significance of the Christian experience and how the indwelling of the Holy

Spirit can direct the life of the individual believer. This belated awareness has been part of the inspiration for "Five Faces of America."

My wife, the former Mary Constance Miller, of Thomasville, Ga., was also reared in a spiritually oriented family. Her mother was the former Anna Dean Knapp, whose family was of German descent. Her father, William J. Miller, was of English and German descent. They were members of Thomasville's First Baptist Church. Her grandmother, Janie Knapp, began telling her about Jesus Christ at the age of two and a half, which started her on a lifelong relationship and walk with Him, although she did not make a formal profession of faith until she was eight years of age.

Connie has a deep spiritual nature and an unwavering respect for all of God's creation, people, animals and flowers. She is never happier than when she is digging in the dirt, planting new flowers to show off His creation. For her, it is a way of worshipping and communing with God and an expression of faith and hope for the future. Walking through our neighborhood, wherever we have lived, she has invariably attracted a following of children and animals, all of whom she knows by name. But, most importantly, she maintains a deep respect and love for people, regardless of who they are or where they are from. And she believes it is incumbent upon every person to say nothing about another unless it is good, believing there is good in everyone.

One of her greatest treasures is a Holy Bible, heavily underlined and noted, which she used in Bible study classes throughout her elementary and high school years. A bible instructor was employed expressly for this purpose by the school system where she attended. Connie also found a communion with God through music, playing and performing for others on the piano, cello and violin.

As a family, our greatest spiritual growth occurred as members of Dawson Memorial Baptist Church in

Birmingham. The mentoring and ministry of Dr. Edgar M. Arendall, long-time, now retired pastor, and his wife, Sarah, and the fellowship of many lifelong friends within the church, had a profound and permanent impact upon our lives. Connie was involved in a number of church programs and ministries, as a teacher in children's Sunday School classes, as a den mother for Cub Scouts, and supporting Boy Scout activities, Women's Missionary Union and other activities. Our sons, Clay, Dane, Jr., Mark and Ashley, participated in Sunday School, graded choir programs, Boy Scouts and other activities. All four were motivated to earn both baccalaureate and advanced degrees, and they continue to live sensitive, spiritually-aware lives.

We have experienced the leadership of the Holy Spirit in our lives and the lives of our family throughout career changes, new opportunities, relocations from one geographic area to another and in meeting the daily challenges of living. Life is a lonely journey at best. And life's relationships are both fragile and fleeting. But, the comfort of having a spiritual compass and companion, through the indwelling of the Holy Spirit, is perhaps the most rewarding aspect of the Christian life. The Holy Spirit has minimized our problems, magnified our joys, and given meaning and purpose to our lives.

Printed in the United States
26219LVS00002B/514-519